# WORDS FOR WORSHIP

# Words for Worship

## Edited by
## Arlene M. Mark

HERALD PRESS
Scottdale, Pennsylvania
Waterloo, Ontario

**Library of Congress Cataloging-in-Publication Data**
Words for worship / edited by Arlene M. Mark.
    p.  cm.
    Includes bibliographical references and index.
    ISBN 0-8361-9037-8
    1. Public worship. 2. Church year. 3. Mennonites—Liturgy—
Texts.  I. Mark, Arlene M.
    BV10.2W66  1995
    264'.097—dc20                      95-12504
                                     CIP

Bible quotations and adaptations are used by permission, all rights
reserved; those by Arlene M. Mark are mostly based on the *New Revised
Standard Version Bible*, copyright 1989, by the Division of Christian
Education of the National Council of the Churches of Christ in the USA;
material may be based on other versions, such as GNB, *Good News Bible*,
copyright © American Bible Society—Old Testament 1976; New
Testament, 1966, 1971, 1976; JB, *The Jerusalem Bible*, copyright © 1966 by
Darton, Longman & Todd, Ltd., and Doubleday, a division of Bantam,
Doubleday, Dell Publishing Group, Inc.; NIV, *The Holy Bible, New
International Version*, copyright © 1973, 1978, 1984 International Bible
Society, Zondervan Bible Publishers. The source of a worship piece is
gratefully acknowledged on the page where it appears and is used by
permission. Please inform the publisher of any omissions or errors.

WORDS FOR WORSHIP
Copyright © 1996 by Herald Press, Scottdale, Pa. 15683
   Published simultaneously in Canada by Herald Press,
   Waterloo, Ont. N2L 6H7. All rights reserved, except as noted above
Library of Congress Catalog Number: 95-12504
International Standard Book Number: 0-8361-9037-8
Printed in the United States of America
Book design by Gwen M. Stamm

10 09 08 07 06 05 04 03 02   10 9 8 7 6 5 4 3 2

To order or request information, please call
1-800-759-4447 (individuals); 1-800-245-7894 (trade)
Website: www.mph.org

*To George,*
*my companion*
*in life's ventures*

# Contents

# Preface

Worship begins with God, ever present, acting on our behalf, always drawing us into goodness. When we assemble, we see God's greatness and we adore. We feel our sinfulness and we confess. We hear God's message and we are changed. We go from worship, having met God and been strengthened for our mission in the world.

Much of our worship response is verbal, for instinctively, words become our vehicle of expression. When we sing, pray, read Scripture, and communicate with each other, words are essential. Of course, no words can substitute for the promptings of the Holy Spirit, nor can printed words supersede the flow of God's voice, speaking in sound and silence.

But words make up the common vehicle by which we convey ideas to each other and to God, so they must be chosen wisely. Our words represent our thoughts. They serve to clarify our assumptions and ideologies. We present ideas forcefully by choosing the best words suited to our purpose.

Words also set the tone of worship. While the primary purpose of worship is always joyful remembrance of God's wonderful acts and our thankful response (and secondarily, edification and teaching directed to the congregation), our words may be heavily preachy, punishing, or penitential, resulting in a lingering sense of guilt and rebuke. What we choose to say reflects our understanding of the purpose of worship. Let there be freshness and vitality to lift our spirits in praise with enough dignity worthy of the purpose of gathering.

Our words of worship shape our thinking and our theology. The words we hear and speak are the seeds of our spiritual food; they form and reform us in fundamental ways. This nourishment promotes the development of our beliefs, the basis of our convictions for action. Many of us identify beliefs from words we've heard or sung. As a child, the Sunday school song, "My God is writing all the time," gave me a distorted concept of an account-keeping, judgmental God. It took many years of teaching and words of good hymnody to move me beyond that limiting, improper image of God.

Words can move us from passivity to involvement. There is no place for an audience in worship. Words in worship provide a means of giving ourselves as participants. Printing words appropriate for the focus of the service unifies a congregation in its quest for God and minimizes quiescence. A printed worship guide also promotes coherence and a sense of flow for the service.

Words for worship need to focus attention on God, Jesus Christ, and the Holy Spirit. These words need to be prepared with honesty of content, appropriateness for the occasion, and clarity of meaning. One cannot ask a congregation to speak words which they do not understand nor commit to statements they do not believe. Worship leaders do well to select words prayerfully and with purpose.

*Words for Worship* offers possibilities for many acts of worship and considers many topics. Its purpose is to promote better worship and provide useful expressions of thought. Thus this collection is offered with the prayer,

> Let the words of my mouth
> and the meditation of my heart
> be acceptable to you,
> O Lord, my rock and my redeemer. (Ps. 19:14)

# Acknowledgments

The book you hold is a collection of worship resources from many writers. Someone requested that I publish materials I had written over the years. To me, this seemed too limiting. When others were informed of the project, many shared their writings. To all those who responded, I am grateful. I also sought sources elsewhere. This collection will not provide for all events and circumstances, but I hope it will be a ready resource on many occasions for busy pastors and worship leaders.

I am indebted to four wonderful people who gave advisory counsel and invaluable guidance. They read and evaluated hundreds of selections. Their expertise improved this book; their encouragement sustained me. Each brought special talents to their work: Helen Alderfer's skills as an editor and writer, Phil Clemens's abilities as pastor and worship leader, Richard Kauffman's knowledge as theologian, and Willard Roth's competent editorial know-how coupled with his persistent confidence in the project—these all moved me along. Thanks to Phil Bedsworth, who first encouraged me to write worship materials for Prairie Street Mennonite Church; to Dan Schrock, whose letter to Herald Press got this project going; and to my editor, S. David Garber, who persisted in ferreting out source information.

Thanks to my son Scott and his wife, Summer, who piloted me through the shoals of computer operation; and to all my family, who gave me support and cheered me along the way.

# Abbreviations

| | |
|---|---|
| 1: | Antiphonal reading by one half of the congregation |
| 2: | Antiphonal reading by other half of the congregation |
| Adapted | Text revised to suit present use |
| *All:* | Leader and people |
| HP | Herald Press, Scottdale, Pa. |
| L: | Leader of the worship |
| MBCM | Mennonite Board of Congregational Ministries, Elkhart, Ind. |
| MBM | Mennonite Board of Missions, Elkhart, Ind. |
| MCC | Mennonite Central Committee, Akron, Pa. |
| MMA | Mennonite Mutual Aid Association, Goshen, Ind. |
| MPH | Mennonite Publishing House, Scottdale, Pa. |
| P: | People gathered to worship |

# "Not Neglecting
to Meet Together"

## *An Order of Worship*

## Gathering

A significant part of worship takes place as Christians simply come together. The community of faith is formed when God's people gather at a common location to separate themselves from their personal space and join together as a covenanted people of Christian. Real people greet each other with words of welcome and encouragement, shake hands, and then assemble to sustain their identity through worship.

Not often do we consider the importance of assembling together. The writer of Hebrews reminds us that to hold fast to our confession of hope, we must not neglect to meet together (10:25). Our worship of God and the nourishing of our faith are not merely solitary experiences. We depend on each other, and gathering is part of the ritual of a people committed to giving and receiving the word and bread of life. We are priests for each other and share together in the word and work of worship. We worship to remind ourselves that together we are the church. We observe how we are fulfilling our calling to be the church. We accord responsibility to each other. We admit our failures together and make new beginnings. We change in each other's presence, for Christian worship changes people. As we meet God, we are being transformed.

The church invites all persons, so we seek to use inclusive

words for worship that are welcoming and understandable. Some of these words may briefly explain actions unfamiliar to newcomers or not well understood by others.

## Call to Worship

Worship is not automatic. It is an act of the will, inspired by the spirit of gratitude. Words that direct our thinking from the mundane will prepare us for the high and holy occupation of divine worship.

An appropriate beginning for worship is an invitation, addressed not to God but to the congregation, to deliberately celebrate God's presence. These words remind us of the lofty purpose for which we have come together. Our thoughts will be directed Godward as we declare God's holiness and are lifted beyond ourselves. ("Good morning" is a personal greeting which does not enhance the focus of worship. It is more suitable in the hallways before worship begins.)

## Invocation

The first prayer, a response to the Call to Worship, is short and well focused. It recognizes the majesty and infinite glory of our omnipotent God. It reminds us that the *primary* purpose of worship is to glorify God and offer praise, not to bless the individual worshiper. (Surely the blessing happens, but as in giving any gift, the focus is not immediately on the giver). The invocation humbly invokes God to assist us in the offering of worship. It does not invite God to come but recognizes that holy God is among us, waiting for our praise. We call upon God for assistance so that worship will be offered to give honor and glory.

# Hymns of Praise

The congregation, called to awe and reverence, is now ready to respond in worship to God. Words of praise sung by the congregation direct our thoughts Godward and remind us that we are in the presence of the Holy. We declare God's lordship. Our affirmations of God's supreme worth provide an assuring foundation for the worship we expect to experience as we move from opening of the service to the climax.

# Confessing and Assurance

When we see ourselves in the light of God's righteousness, we know we must deal honestly with the sin in our lives. If we cherish sin, our worship is not acceptable to God (Ps. 66:18). Telling God our sin is not informing God of anything; our holy God already knows. But the presence of evil keeps us from kinship with God, and worshipers need the opportunity to have this barrier removed.

Corporate statements of confession are the prayer of the people and should be said in unison. The household of God names our social, corporate, and systemic sin that hurts our whole world. Our words are a public testimony of our participation in the sins of society. We hold before us a corporate mirror of honesty and refuse to excuse our behavior by rationalizing it.

Bidding prayers, which encourage individuals during moments of silence to seek forgiveness, are soul-searching. Responsive readings, hymns, or songs of confession are other ways to confess sin.

Through confession, God's penitent people become intimately aware of guilt. Hence, they need to be reminded that a gracious God has given assurance of full forgiveness through pardoning grace. God alone can forgive, but the sin-burdened soul should be assured of God's forgiveness through Christ.

## Praying

**1.** The first prayer is of adoration, and the second prayer is of confession. If a prayer of confession is not used, confession should be part of the pastoral prayer.

**2.** Prayers of thanksgiving should not be reserved for one special holiday a year. In adoration, we focus on who God is; in thanksgiving, we remember what God has done and is doing. Gratitude reminds us of the benefits we enjoy and leaves us indebted to a generous God.

**3.** The pastoral prayer begins with words of praise, adoration, or thanksgiving but is largely intercession (praying for others) and petition (praying for ourselves). Often this prayer comes after the sermon and gathers together the concerns of the morning. It serves to enlarge vision and includes not only the congregation but also looks outward to the community and the world. The pastoral prayer puts into eternal perspective the events of the past week and those of the coming week.

Prayer of intercession is conversation with God, not magic. It is not getting what we want with push-button speed. Prayer is a means of getting what God wants. It should always be in the attitude of Jesus' prayer to his Father: "Yet, not what I want, but what you want" (Mark 14:36). When we ask God to intervene in problems of our lives and our world, we must accept that God often does these things through us. We are offering ourselves to participate in God's active love and not dictating to God what must happen. Intercession can be powerful when it moves us to do what we ask in prayer; it dare not be manipulation of God.

## Proclaiming

### 1. Scripture

The function of synagogue worship was to listen to Scripture reading and hear it interpreted in the context of the times. Today, Scripture is still the basis of instruction for surviving in an alien world. Lectionaries provide a psalm and three Scripture readings, which often suggest a sermon theme. Whether or not the lectionary is used, the Bible, the record of God's redemptive action, must be read because God's people need to hear God's Word. Listening to the story gives us a sense of God in our history. "Return" and "remember" are words frequently used to give a perspective of larger purpose and meaning to life today. Scripture provides a vision of a world as it ought to be and gives us new ways of thinking. Scripture is our canon for judging between faithfulness and falling away. It calls us back to discipleship. It is our source of encouragement and hope. Therefore, let us hear Scripture texts—read well—as proclamation from God.

Scripture passages direct our focus for the sermon and should immediately precede the sermon. The version which provides the most clarity, beauty, and reliability should be chosen. Let the Word come alive.

### 2. Sermon

The sermon is the proclamation of the authoritative Word of God for today and builds up the body of Christ, the church. While we no longer assume that the sermon is the whole point of the service, most of worship has focused us to receive the message for our contemporary world. Through the interpretation of the Scriptures, God is revealed to us and we see ourselves in God's light. The test of worship becomes our response to the call to change, to learn how to follow Jesus in daily life.

## Response

Following the sermon, a corporate response is appropriate. This might be a hymn of dedication, an affirmation of faith, a responsive reading, or another act of commitment to the message received.

# Sending

Worshipers should be dismissed with the assurance that the power and presence of God accompanies them always. The blessing, or benediction, is the spoken word of promise that God goes with us as we depart. The Christian goes out from worship, carrying a message of God's reign to give to the world. God goes with us; so does the command of Christ to make disciples of all, and our Lord's promise, "Remember, I am with you always" (Matt. 28:20).

# Optional Placement in Order of Worship

## 1. Offering

The receiving of gifts and offerings is not optional, but the placing of it in the worship service may be. Some congregations prefer to have it in the early part of worship as a response of adoration. Others place it following the sermon as a response to the message. Certainly, if the sermon is on stewardship, the offering would appropriately follow.

Wherever it occurs in the service, worshipers should know that the offering is an act of pure worship. The offering is the link between our words and our acts; between our daily labors and our spiritual commitment. Jesus told us that our hearts are closely connected with our finances; in the offering we put our money where our words are.

When there is offertory music, it should not detract from the worship of giving. The music itself should be an offering, not a performance, and the musicians should no more receive applause than the preacher (or any other leader in the service).

When the gifts are carried to the front of the sanctuary, the congregation may rise to sing the doxology. Or a prayer may be offered on behalf of the congregation as a blessing of the gifts.

## 2. Affirmation of Faith

Anabaptist churches are not creedal, and corporate faith affirmations are not seen as the main basis for membership beliefs. However, the stating of the church's teachings will help people examine their own commitment. The congregation benefits from reading together the words of faith they hold in common. In an age of uncertain theology, confessions of faith identify core Christian teachings. These will also serve from time to time as teaching devices for new believers.

## 3. Announcements and Sharing Time

The primary purpose of coming to worship is to glorify God, not to communicate personal concerns. Bulletins should carry most of the announcements; yet worshipers may need to voice a few last-minute items of profound interest to the total congregation. Sharing time should major on matters that concern our spiritual life together and not impair the dignity of the service nor detract from our worship of God.

## 4. Children's Time

Communicating the message of the morning to children is important. When we take time to explain to children on their level of understanding, we indicate their importance both as persons and as learners of the faith. Coming just before the sermon, the Children's Time serves to prepare their (and the congregation's) minds for the essence of the message and encourages listening for particular ideas. This should be viewed as a teachable moment, focused on Scripture, and captivating enough to hold attention and open up age-appropriate meaning.

## 5. Music

During the course of the service, there will be opportunities for singing. Nothing unites a congregation as well as good singing, and nothing separates one out so quickly as not being able to participate. Selections should be chosen with the congregation's ability in mind, or there should be provision made for accompaniment to assist in learning tunes and harmony.

Music should also be chosen because of its message. Great hymns of the ages are a repository of deep devotion and praise to God. When we express the sentiment of their words, we immediately have God uppermost in our minds.

Some music used in church services focuses primarily on the individual and a wish for self-growth and security. This is not an appropriate corporate response to the loving presence of God.

Consider the content of the songs. There are hymns which are suitable for any point in the sequence of the service. Careful worship planning will include many selections which heighten the progression of the service and serve to unify the service as a whole.

## 6. Passing the Peace

Exchanging words such as "The peace of God be with you," "May God give you peace," or simply "Peace" is an opportunity for greeting each other with handshakes or hugs. This helps us reach out to those we know and those we want to know. We are a community, seeking God together, being agents of reconciliation and encouragement both in the pews and in the world beyond the pews.

Christians gather in worship, not chiefly to sing moving songs or hear compelling sermons, but to respond in devotion to God. In our gathering, Christians participate in these actions for spiritual growth: speaking and listening, singing and silence, giving and receiving.

These actions reaffirm our loyalty to God, renew our commitment to Christ's teachings, and respond to the Holy Spirit's promptings. Worship's primary purpose is to give glory to God. Worship ought also to give direction to all of life. Worship leaders, song leaders, and pastors need to coordinate their planning so that worshipers encounter the holiness of God and embrace the vision of what earthly realities might become.

# WORDS FOR WORSHIP

# The Christian Year

## Advent

### 1 Call to Worship

L: As quietly as the winter steals upon us,
　　the season of joy approaches.
**P: We wait for our Redeemer,**
　　**for God's love to come in fullness.**
L: The day is coming quickly;
　　the God of mystery draws near.
**P: Therefore we wait expectantly,**
　　**attentive to all the signs of his coming.**
*All: Come quickly, Lord Jesus!*

—Diane Karay, *All the Seasons of Mercy* (© 1987 Diane Karay; used by permission of Westminster John Knox Press), 13 (adapted). Based on Luke 21:25-36; Rev. 22:20

### 2 Call to Worship

L: Come, let us praise the Lord.
**P: Let our spirits rejoice in God our Savior.**
L: The Mighty One has done great things for us;
　　Holy is God's name.

P: **God's mercy extends to those who honor him
  from generation to generation.**

L: God has brought down powerful rulers
  and lifted the humble.

P: **God has filled the hungry with good things
  and sent the rich away empty.**

*All: Let us magnify the Lord
  and rejoice in God our Savior.*

—Arlene M. Mark, in MPH Bulletin, 12-18-84. Based on Luke 1:46-55

# 3 Call to Worship

*(correlate with no 8)*

L: Let us hear the revelation of God's promise,

P: **for Advent is a time of expecting new light to shine.**

L: Let us receive light from the prophets,

P: **for light penetrates darkness and prepares the way
  of the Lord.**

L: Let us see God's glory shine forth,

P: **for we long to be transformed
  by the light of God's holiness.**

—Arlene M. Mark, in MPH Bulletin, 11-27-88

# 4 Call to Worship

L: Be strong, and let your heart take courage,
  all you who wait for the Lord.

P: **For lo, I will come and dwell in your midst,
  says the Lord.**

L: Many nations shall join themselves to the Lord on that day,
  and shall be my people;
  and I will dwell in their midst.

P: **Then the glory of the Lord shall be revealed,
  and all people shall see it together,**

for the mouth of the Lord has spoken it.
*All:  God's kingdom is an everlasting kingdom,*
        *God's dominion endures through all generations.*
        *The Lord is faithful in all his words,*
            *and gracious in all his deeds.*

—Arlene M. Mark, in MPH Bulletin, 11-28-82. Based on Ps. 31:24; Zech. 2:10-11;
    Isa. 40:5; Ps. 145:13

# 5  Call to Worship

Hear the invitation of the prophet Isaiah:
    Come, let us go up to God's holy mountain,
        that we may learn to walk in all God's ways.
    For God will judge between the nations,
        and shall decide for many peoples.
    And they shall beat their swords into plowshares,
        and their spears into pruning hooks.
    Nation shall not lift up sword against nation,
        neither shall they learn war any more.
    Let us come before God and learn God's ways of peace.

—Ruth C. Duck, in *Touch Holiness*, ed. by Ruth C. Duck and Maren C. Tirabassi
    (Cleveland: Pilgrim Press, 1990), 3. Based on Isa. 2:3-4

# 6  Call to Worship

L: Let us hear what God the Lord will speak,
        for God will speak peace to his people.
**P: God will speak peace to the faithful,**
        **to those who turn to him in their hearts.**
L: Surely, God's salvation is at hand
        for those who fear him,
        that his glory may dwell in our land.
**P: Steadfast love and faithfulness will meet;**
        **righteousness and peace will kiss each other.**
L: The Lord will give what is good,

and our land will yield its increase.
**P: Righteousness will go before the Lord,
and prepare the path for him.
Let us prepare the way for the Lord.**

—Arlene M. Mark. Based on Ps. 85:8-13

# 7 Invocation

O God,
we praise you in our worship today
that Mary responded to your Spirit
and was your servant to bring salvation.
Let us give ourselves also, as your servants;
let us be bearers of good news
and messengers of mercy and peace,
through Christ we pray. Amen.

—Arlene M. Mark, in MPH Bulletin, 12-18-84. Based on Luke 1:46-55

# 8 Invocation
*(correlate with no. 3)*

We come, our God, seeking light:
light to reveal your majesty;
light to clear our blindness;
light to illumine our understanding.
Come into our hearts and lives as we worship,
so that we may serve in your kingdom as bearers of light
and guide others to the Light.
In Jesus' name we pray. Amen.

—Arlene M. Mark, in MPH Bulletin, 11-27-88

# 9 Advent Prayer

God our deliverer,
>whose approaching birth
>still shakes the foundations of our world,
>may we so wait for your coming
>with eagerness and hope
>that we embrace without terror
>the labor pangs of the new age
>through Jesus Christ. Amen.

—Janet Morley, *All Desires Known* (Wilton, Conn.: Morehouse-Barlow, 1989), 9.
Based on Luke 1:51-53; Rom. 8:18-25

# 10 Prayer for Light

O Christ,
>we watch and wait
>>for the warmth and light of your presence.
>As candlelight overcomes the darkness,
>>so your light radiates within us
>>and warms the wintry seasons of our lives.
>We live with hope
>>that the good news of your coming
>>will warm and brighten every heart
>>and the world will fall to its knees in joy. Amen.

—Diane Karay, *All the Seasons of Mercy* (© 1987 Diane Karay; used by permission
of Westminster John Knox Press), 17 (adapted)

# 11 Prayer for Peace

God of holy peace,
>we are accustomed to the darkness of our world,
>>accustomed to tragedy, sorrow, worry.
>Like the shepherds sitting in darkness, expecting nothing,
>>we are familiar with dim hope.

Yet we brood over our troubled lives and wicked world,
  wondering when you will come in power
  to bring peace to all hearts and lands.
Break the grip of darkness;
  let your peace dawn in our hearts!
Look with favor upon your people;
  grant your blessing.
Should angels bring clear messages for our lives,
  let us with wonder accept your news of love
  as the generous gift it is. Amen.

—Diane Karay, *All the Seasons of Mercy* (© 1987 Diane Karay; used by permission of Westminster John Knox Press), 25 (adapted)

# 12 Lighting of the Advent Wreath

*The Advent wreath is a simple circle of evergreens, a sign of life without end. Four purple candles are arranged among the greens with an additional white candle centered in the middle, called the Christ candle. The wreath is placed on a table at the front of the church. A candle is lighted on the first Sunday of the Advent season, and an additional candle is lighted each Sunday. Candles may need to be replaced. On Christmas Day, all the candles of Advent and the white center candle are lighted. The center candle can be saved and used again on Easter as a reminder of the connection between these two events of salvation.*

### First Sunday of Advent

L: We wait for light,
    and lo! there is darkness;
  we long for brightness,
    but we walk in gloom.
*All: As we prepare to greet the Light,*
    *let our blinded eyes be opened,*
    *for Christ is the light to them*
      *that sit in darkness.*
L: Let us pray:

O God of light,
    we wander in the darkness of despair
        and long for a better way.
    Increase our desire for Christ's coming;
        strengthen our waiting with purpose.
    Let your light shine before us
        and lead us in this time of expectation. Amen.
*(Light a purple candle.)*

### Second Sunday of Advent

L: The unfolding of God's word gives light;
    it imparts understanding to the simple.
*All:  As we wait for the living light,*
    *let us hear God's word*
      *and live by Christ's teachings.*
L: Let us pray:
  Mighty God,
    Light of the world,
      shine in our hearts;
    let your words of wisdom
      teach us the way of salvation.
    Come with grace and mercy
      to cleanse our hearts for living light. Amen.
*(Light two purple candles.)*

### Third Sunday of Advent

L: The Lord is our light and our salvation,
    whom shall we fear?
  The Lord is the stronghold of our life;
    of whom shall we be afraid?
*All:  As we long for the light,*
    *let us lay aside every weight*
      *and the sin that clings so closely.*
    *Let us be glad and rejoice*
      *in the Lord's salvation.*

L: Let us pray:
  Eternal God,
    you are our salvation, our strength, our shield.
   In this season of expectancy,
     open our eyes to our sin.
  Let your Spirit reveal the darkness of our souls;
    let daybreak come through your deliverance.
  Come in the glory of your saving light
    and shine upon our pathways. Amen.
*(Light three purple candles.)*

## Fourth Sunday of Advent

L: The time is fulfilled,
  the kingdom of God has come near;
  the true light which enlightens everyone
    is coming into the world.

*All: As we anticipate the light,*
    *let us be alert and watching*
      *for the glorious appearing*
      *of our God and Savior, Jesus Christ.*

L: Let us pray:
  O Lord our God,
    the night is far spent,
      and the day is at hand.
    Keep us observant, watching
      for the coming of your Son,
        in whom is light to reflect your splendor.
  Come and lead us to joy and peace. Amen.
*(Light all four purple candles.)*

## Christmas Sunday

L: Arise, shine; for God's light has come,
    and the glory of the Lord has risen upon us.
  Nations shall come to this light,
    and kings to the brightness of this dawn.

*All:  Let us rejoice;*
*the splendid eternal light*
*shines on all who live in darkness,*
*and Christ has come*
*to witness to that light.*

L:  Let us pray:
God of promise,
the coming of your Son into the world
has revealed your glory.
Salvation is nearer to us now
than when we became believers.
Let us lay aside the works of darkness
and put on the armor of light;
let us live honorably as in the day.
Let us live simply and devoutly,
set apart as your people
who have seen the light. Amen.
*(Light all four Advent candles and the Christ candle.)*

—Arlene M. Mark. Based on Matt. 4:16; Eph. 5:14; Pss. 119:130; 27:1; Heb. 12:1;
Isa. 25:9; John 1:9; Titus 2:13; Isa. 60:1-3; Rom. 13:11-13; Isa. 59:9b; Luke 1:79

## Christmas Season

## 13 Call to Worship

L:  I bring you good news:
let your hearts be joyful,
let your spirits rejoice.

P:  **The newborn child is the Savior of the world,**
**the incarnation of the holy God,**
**come among us.**

L:  Those who walk in darkness
will see the shining light.

P: **Those who suffer the yoke of oppression**
    **will be set free.**

All: *For a child has been born:*
    *authority rests upon his shoulders,*
    *and there shall be endless peace.*
   *He will establish his kingdom*
    *and uphold it with justice and righteousness*
    *from this time onward and forever.*
   *Our hearts are joyful,*
    *our spirits rejoice,*
    *for the child-Christ who has come,*
    *lives and reigns*
    *with God above, now and eternally.*

—Arlene M. Mark. Based on Isa. 9:2-7; Matt. 4:16

# 14  Call to Worship

L: Behold, I give you good tidings of great joy;
    Christ the Lord is born today.

P: **How beautiful on the mountains**
    **are the feet of those**
    **who bring good news.**

L: Break forth together into singing,
    for the Lord has comforted his people,
    the Lord has redeemed Jerusalem.

P: **The people who walked in darkness**
    **have seen a great light;**
   **those who lived in a land of deep darkness—**
    **on them has the light shined.**

All: *The prophets' promises are made flesh*
    *before the eyes of all the nations;*
   *all the ends of the earth shall see*
    *the salvation of our God.*

> **Glory to God in the highest heaven,**
> **and on earth, peace and goodwill among all. Amen.**

—Arlene M. Mark. Based on Isa. 52:7-10; 9:2; Luke 2

# 15 Christmas Prayer

Eternal God,
> Ruler of all worlds and Shepherd of the stars,
> your glory is revealed in vastness and in power,
> > yet your greatest name is Love.
> This is the time we remember your gentleness,
> > hidden in a mother's hope.
> This is the time we believe again
> > that love is stronger than fear,
> > that peace is stronger than hate,
> > that darkness will never conquer the light.
> In this season of God-with-us,
> > we offer our gift of gratitude
> > and we make bold to believe
> > that we are graced with your presence,
> > for we are gathered in the name of love. Amen.

—David Beebe, in *Flames of the Spirit*, ed. by Ruth C. Duck (Cleveland: Pilgrim Press, 1985), 24 (adapted)

# 16 Prayer of Confession

Redeeming God,
> you are waiting with us,
> > for we are slow to make room
> > in our hearts for the Christ child.
> Your stars are shining,
> > and the angels' songs are praising.
> Yet we are in no hurry
> > to hear the message of peace and goodwill,

to sing "Glory" with the angels,
to leave our sheep on the hillside,
and come with haste to find incarnation.
Redeeming God,
forgive our unbelief,
forgive our lack of wonder,
forgive our denying the birth in our midst.
Open us to your miracle;
let us hear again the message of love
that Jesus Christ is born.
Let us respond with joyous hearts,
glorifying and praising God
for all that we have heard and seen. Amen.

—Arlene M. Mark

# 17 Prayer of Adoration

Glory to you, almighty God,
for you sent your only-begotten Son,
that we might have new life.
Glory to you, Lord Jesus Christ,
for you became flesh and dwelt among us,
that we might become your people.
Glory to you, Holy Spirit,
for you are the promised gift,
that we might witness in power.
Glory to you, almighty God,
and to your Son, Jesus Christ,
and to the Holy Spirit,
now and forever. Amen.

—*Liturgical Year,* Supplemental Liturgical Resource 7 (Louisville: Westminster/ John Knox Press, © 1992; used by permission of Westminster John Knox Press), 73, from *Book of Common Worship* (Presbyterian Church, USA, 1946; adapted)

# Epiphany Season

## 18 Call to Worship

L: O magnify the Lord with me,
   and let us exalt God's name together.

**P: From the rising of the sun to its setting,**
   **the name of the Lord be praised!**

L: Nations shall come to the light,
   and kings to the brightness of God's dawn.

**P: They shall bring gold and frankincense,**
   **and shall proclaim the praise of the Lord.**
   **Arise, shine; for our light has come,**
   **and the glory of the Lord**
   **has risen upon us. Amen.**

—Arlene M. Mark. Based on Ps. 113:3; Isa. 60

## 19 Call to Worship

L: With one voice, let us glorify
   the God and Father
   of our Lord Jesus Christ.

**P: We will speak of the glory of God's kingdom,**
   **and tell of God's power.**

L: The Son is the radiance of God's glory,
   and he is the manifestation of the Father.

**P: In Christ, the complete being**
   **of the Godhead dwells.**

L: The incarnation of Christ
   has brought the divine
   into our midst.

**P: God's love was revealed among us in this way;**
   **God sent his only Son into the world,**
   **so that we might live through him. Amen.**

—Arlene M. Mark. Based on Rom. 15:6; Ps. 145:11; Col. 2:9; 1 John 4:9

## 20  Call to Worship

L: Let the name of the Lord be praised,
    both now and forever.

**P: For God has anointed Jesus of Nazareth**
    **with the Holy Spirit and with power,**

L: to preach good news to the poor,
    to proclaim freedom for the captives,

**P: to release the oppressed,**
    **to proclaim the year of the Lord's favor.**

L: At Jesus' baptism, God confirmed,
    "This is my Son, whom I love;
    with whom I am well pleased."

**P: Let us praise God**
    **that Jesus was baptized to fulfill all righteousness,**
    **that we are buried with Christ in baptism,**
    **that we will be united with Christ in resurrection. Amen.**

—Arlene M. Mark. Based on Matt. 3:11, 13-17; Luke 4:18-21; Rom. 6:4

## 21  Epiphany Invocation

O God, Ruler of times and seasons,
    in every change you fulfill your steady purpose of grace.
    Beneath all that now in winter seems dark and cold,
        you are keeping safe the hidden germs of life.
        You are preparing the days when the earth shall bud
            and bring forth again her harvest.
    Teach us by your course in nature
        to trust you in your dealings with us.
        Preserve in us the seed of that life
        which is life indeed.
    With your light and strength,
        carry on the work of your grace in us

and visit us with your salvation;
>through Jesus Christ our Lord. Amen.

—R. Crompton Jones, in *The Narrow Way* (London: J. Whitaker & Sons, Ltd.;
adapted)

## 22 Prayer for Epiphany

Almighty God,
>your holy love descended to us
>in the person of Jesus.
>Christ's baptism revealed him
>to be your blessed Son.
>Christ's life revealed to us
>the way to your righteousness.
>Anoint us by your Spirit
>that we may live faithful to your calling,
>and you may be known as love
>throughout all the world. Amen.

—Arlene M. Mark

## 23 Prayer for Transfiguration Sunday

God of glory and mercy,
>before his death in shame,
>your Son went to the mountaintop,
>and you revealed his life in glory.
Where prophets witnessed to him,
>you proclaimed him your Son,
>but he returned to die among us.
Help us face evil with courage,
>knowing that all things, even death,

are subject to your transforming power.
We ask this through Christ our Lord. Amen.

—James F. White, from *Seasons of the Gospel* (© 1979 by Abingdon; used by
permission) p. 67 (adapted)

# Lent

## 24 Call to Worship

L: Rend your hearts and not your clothing.
　　Return to the Lord, your God,

**P: for the Lord is gracious and merciful,
　　slow to anger,
　　and abounding in steadfast love.**

L: Even now, says the Lord,
　　return to me with all your heart,

**P: with fasting, with weeping,
　　and with mourning.**

*All: When the righteous cry for help,
　　the Lord hears,
　　and rescues them from all their troubles. Amen.*

—Arlene M. Mark. Based on Joel 2:12-13; Ps. 34:17

## 25 Call to Worship

L: Come, all who are weary
　　and carrying heavy burdens,
　　and Christ will give rest.

**P: Those who wait for the Lord
　　shall renew their strength,
　　they shall mount up with wings like eagles.**

L: The Lord is always before us.
　　Because God is at our right hand,
　　we shall not be moved.

P: God shows us the path of life.
   In God's presence there is fullness of joy;
   in God's right hand are pleasures forevermore.
*All: Therefore our hearts are glad,*
   *our souls rejoice;*
   *our bodies rest secure.*

—Arlene M. Mark. Based on Matt. 11:28; Isa. 40:31; Ps. 16:8-11

## 26 Call to Worship

1: Come
      out of moments of despair,
      out of moments of joy,
      out of your everydays,
      out of heights, out of depths.
   Come as you are.
   Come, worship
      the One who loves us.
*2: We come*
      *to wait for the One who redeems us.*
   *We wait for the Lord.*
*All: O wait for the Lord.*

—Linea Reimer Geiser, Goshen, Ind.

## 27 Call to Worship

1: Come nearer to God;
      return from the far country,
      from self-exile,
      from selfish desire.
   God awaits our return.
*2: God meets us on the way;*
      *God's arms are open to welcome us.*

1: God welcomes the lost
   and celebrates our return.
*All: Let us worship our God,*
     *whose lavish love awaits our homecoming,*
     *who rejoices when the lost is found.*

—Arlene M. Mark. Based on Luke 15:1-3, 11-32

## 28 Call to Worship

L: O come, let us sing to the Lord.
**P: Let us make a joyful noise**
    **to the rock of our salvation.**
L: God proves his love for us
   in that while we were still sinners,
   Christ died for us.
**P: God's love has been poured into our hearts**
    **like a gushing spring of water,**
    **like water from a rock.**
L: We come into God's presence with thanksgiving,
   making a joyful noise
   with songs of praise.
*All: We worship in spirit and in truth.*

—Ruth Yoder, MBCM Lenten Worship Res. (1993). Based on Ps. 95; John 4:5-26;
Rom. 5:1-11; Exod. 17:3-7

## 29 Call to Worship

L: Seek the Lord while he may be found;
   call on him while he is near.
**P: Let the wicked forsake their way,**
    **and the unrighteous their thoughts;**
L: let them return to the Lord,
   that he may have mercy on them,

P: **and to our God,**
**for he will abundantly pardon.**
*All: Blessed be the Lord,*
*who daily bears us up;*
*God is our salvation.*

—Arlene M. Mark. Based on Isa. 55:6-7; Ps. 68:19

# 30 Call to Worship

L: Come now, let us reason together,
says the Lord:
though your sins are like scarlet,
they shall be like snow;

P: **though they are red like crimson,**
**they shall become like wool.**

L: Happy are those whose transgression
is forgiven,
whose sin is covered.

P: **Happy are those to whom the Lord**
**imputes no iniquity,**
**and in whose spirit**
**there is no deceit.**

—Arlene M. Mark. Based on Isa. 1:18; Ps. 32:1-2

# 31 Prayer

Most holy God,
your Son came to serve sinners.
We come to this season of repentance,
confessing our sinfulness,
asking for new and honest hearts,
and the healing power of your forgiveness.
Grant this through Christ our Lord. Amen.

—The English translation of the prayer from *The Roman Missal* (© 1973,
International Committee on English in the Liturgy, Inc. All rights reserved)

## 32 Prayer

Our God of infinite love and compassion,
    we bless and praise you.
    When we stray, you patiently await our return.
    When we return, you welcome us.
    When you welcome us, you forgive our sins
    and heal us to wholeness.
    We bless and praise you,
    our God of health and salvation.

—Arlene M. Mark

## 33 Lenten Call to Prayer

In this Lenten season, O God,
    we come before you,
    asking for courage to open our eyes.
We want to see ourselves as you see us:
    the empty and barren places,
    the halfhearted struggles,
    the faint stirrings of new life.
We come, trusting your grace,
    waiting for your illuminating word,
    longing for your healing light.
Do not let us be blind to your presence.
Shine upon us, O God,
    and make our paths clear,
    for we pray in the name of Jesus. Amen.

—Marlene Kropf, Elkhart, Ind.

## 34 Prayer of Confession

L: Our God,
we are thirsty people.
Our hearts are parched from wandering
in the desert of sin,
far from your life-giving springs.
Call us to your well.

**P: Fill our cups with your grace.
Let your love overflow in our hearts,
and make us come fully alive. Amen.**

—Ruth Yoder, MBCM Lenten Worship Res. (1993; adapted). Based on John 4:5-
26; Exod. 17:3-7

## 35 Prayer of Repentance

1: Lord, I have denied you
by refusing to know you.

2: I have betrayed you
by keeping my distance.

1: I have mocked you
by pretending I am not yours.

2: Lord, I am lost;
let your forgiveness find me.

1: Forgive my following afar;
take away my self-sufficiency.

2: Welcome me into your strong, forgiving arms,
and let me feel reconciled again.

*All: Receive me as a penitent child
returning to you.
Let the old pass away,
let all things be made new.
Change me from betrayer to friend,
and give me the task*

> *of making others friends.*
> *In the name of your forgiving Son, Amen.*

—Arlene M. Mark. Based on Luke 15:11-32; 2 Cor. 5:16-21; Matt. 26:69-75

## 36  Prayer of Lament

1:  Out of the depths of despair I cry to you,
  O Lord.
  Lord, hear my cry for help!
  Let your ears listen
  to the voice of my pleading.

2:  If you, O Lord, should record our guilt,
  who could escape condemnation?
  But there is forgiveness with you,
  so that you will be revered.

1:  I wait for the Lord with all my heart,
  and in God's word, I trust.
  My soul longs for the Lord
  more than those who watch eagerly for dawn.

2:  Hope in the Lord!
  For with the Lord there is love unfailing
  and willingness to save.
  God is the one who redeems all people
  from their sins.

—Arlene M. Mark. Based on Ps. 130

## 37  Responsive Reading and Prayer

L:  Happy are those whose sins are forgiven,
  whose wrongs are pardoned.

**P:  Happy is the one whom the Lord**
  **does not accuse of doing wrong**
  **and who is free from all deceit.**

L: When I did not confess my sins,
　　I was worn out from crying all day long.

**P: Day and night God's hand was heavy upon me;**
　　**my strength was completely drained,**
　　**as moisture is dried by summer heat.**

L: Then I confessed my sins;
　　I did not conceal my wrongdoings.

**P: I decided to confess my transgressions,**
　　**and God forgave the guilt of my sin.**

### Prayer

L: Be merciful to me, O God, because of your constant love.

**P: Because of your great mercy, wipe away my sins.**

L: Wash away all my evil, and make me clean from my sins.

**P: Wash me and I shall be whiter than snow.**

*All: Let me hear the sounds of joy and gladness*
　　　*and I will be happy once again.*
　　　*Give me again the joy that comes from your salvation,*
　　　*and make me willing to obey you. Amen.*

—Arlene M. Mark. Based on Pss. 32:1-4; 51; GNB

## 38  Call to Worship for Palm Sunday

L: Rejoice greatly, O people of Zion!
　　Shout, children of Jerusalem!

**P: See, your king comes to you,**
　　**righteous and having salvation,**
　　**gentle and riding on a donkey,**
　　**on the colt of a donkey.**

L: Now is Jesus Christ glorified,
　　and God is glorified in him.

**P: Hosanna to the Son of David.**
　　**Blessed is the one who comes**

**in the name of the Lord.**
*All: Hosanna in the highest!*

—Lombard (Ill.) Mennonite Church Bulletin, 4-8-90. Based on Matt. 21; Zech. 9:9; John 13:31

# 39 Confession of Faith

We confess our faith in Jesus Christ,
    who, being divine,
    did not cling to his equality with God,
    but humbled himself as a servant,
    and became obedient to death—
    even death on a cross.
We confess our hope in Christ's exaltation;
    we look forward with joyful expectation to the day
    when every knee will bow,
    and every tongue will confess
    that Jesus Christ is Lord,
    to the glory of God, our Maker.

—Marlene Kropf, Elkhart, Ind., in MPH Bulletin, 3-24-91. Based on Phil. 2:5-11

# 40 Gathering Words for Maundy Thursday

L: This is the day
    that Christ the Lamb of God
    gave himself into the hands of those who would slay him.
**P: This is the day**
    **that Christ gathered with his disciples in the upper room.**
L: This is the day
    that Christ took a towel and washed the disciples' feet,
    giving us an example that we should do to others
    as he has done to us.

P: **This is the day**
  **that Christ our God gave us the holy feast,**
  **that we who eat this bread and drink this cup**
  **may here proclaim his holy sacrifice,**
  **and be partakers of his resurrection,**
  **and at the last day may reign with him in heaven.**

—*Liturgical Year,* Supplemental Liturgical Resource 7 (Louisville: Westminster/
John Knox Press, © 1992; used by permission of Westminster John Knox
Press), 160

# 41 Service of Tenebrae

*This service of readings is an adaptation of an early twelfth-century ser-vice traditionally used in Holy Week. The name Tenebrae (darkness) de-rives from the practice of extinguishing one of the eight candles during each Scripture reading until there is total darkness. This symbolizes the growing despair of Christ as the time for crucifixion draws near. Appro-priate hymn verses may be sung between readings. After the readings, the congregation departs in silence, maintaining the spirit of solemnity in commemoration of the darkness of soul which Christ experienced.*

### Tenebrae Readings

| | |
|---|---|
| 1. Shadow of betrayal | Matthew 26:20-25 |
| 2. Shadow of denial | Matthew 26:31-35 |
| 3. Shadow of resignation | Luke 22:39-44 |
| 4. Shadow of abandonment | Mark 14:32-42 |
| 5. The arrest | John 18:2-12 |
| 6. The trial | Matthew 27:1-2, 11-26 |
| 7. The denial | Mark 14:66-72 |
| 8. Shadow of the cross<br>*darkness and silence . . .* | Mark 15:16-20 |

## 42 Responsive Reading for Good Friday

1: See, my servant shall prosper;
>    he shall be exalted and lifted up,
>    and shall be very high.

2: Just as there were many who were astonished at him
>    —so marred was his appearance, beyond human
>    semblance,
>        and his form beyond that of mortals—
>    so he shall startle many nations;
>        kings shall shut their mouths because of him;
>    for that which had not been told them they shall see,
>    and that which they had not heard they shall contemplate.

1: Who has believed what we have heard?
>        And to whom has the arm of the Lord been revealed?
>    For he grew up before him like a young plant,
>        and like a root out of dry ground;
>    he had no form or majesty that we should look at him.

2: He was despised and rejected by others;
>        a man of suffering and acquainted with infirmity;
>    and as one from whom others hide their faces
>        he was despised, and we held him of no account.

1: Surely he has borne our infirmities
>        and carried our sorrows;
>    yet we accounted him stricken,
>        struck down by God, and afflicted.

2: He was wounded for our transgressions,
>        crushed for our iniquities;
>    upon him was the punishment that made us whole,
>        and by his bruises we are healed.

*All: All we like sheep have gone astray;*
>    *we have turned to our own way,*
>    *and the Lord has laid on him the iniquity of us all.*

*He was oppressed, and he was afflicted,*
  *yet he did not open his mouth;*
*like a lamb that is led to the slaughter,*
  *and like a sheep that is silent before its shearers,*
  *so he did not open his mouth.*
*By a perversion of justice he was taken away.*

1: Who could have imagined his future?
     For he was cut off from the land of the living,
     stricken for the transgression of my people.

2: They made his grave with the wicked
     and his tomb with the rich,
     although he had done no violence,
     and there was no deceit in his mouth.
   Yet it was the will of the Lord to crush him with pain.

1: When you make his life an offering for sin,
     he shall see his offspring,
     and shall prolong his days.
   Out of his anguish he shall see light;
     the righteous one shall make many righteous,
     and shall bear their iniquities.

2: Therefore I will allot him a portion with the great
     because he poured out himself to death,
     and was numbered with the transgressors;
   yet he bore the sin of many,
     and made intercession for the transgressors.

—Based on Isa. 52:13—53:12

## 43 Prayer

O Christ, the Master Carpenter
    who at the last, through wood and nails,
        purchased our whole salvation,
wield well your tools in the workshop of your world,
    so that we, who come rough-hewn to your bench,
        may here be fashioned to a truer beauty of your hand.
We ask it for your own name's sake. Amen.

—*The Iona Community Worship Book* (Glasgow: Wild Goose, 1987), 98; translation
  from German © Iona Community, Glasgow G51 3UU, Scotland

## 44 Prayer

God of all our days,
    on this day when the sun was darkened
      and the earth trembled,
      we remember your suffering.
    We see you as the one forgotten, the one oppressed,
      the one rejected.
    On this day we hear your blood crying out from the ground.
    We hear also the blood of our sisters and brothers
      crying out from Israel and Ireland,
      Nicaragua and El Salvador.
    We see you in your children
      murdered in Central America and South Africa.
    We feel you in the pain of the homeless poor,
      in the senselessness of starving populations,
      in the wounds and death of armed conflict.

We come penitent and sorrowful on the Dark Friday,
    this day of murder and desertion.
We acknowledge that we are not innocent.
We share in the evils of the world
    for we have caused pain to others and ourselves.

We confess the need of your love
    that has borne our griefs
    and carried our sorrows.
You know what it is to be forsaken
    and you understand pain.
Have mercy on us, we pray
    in the name of Jesus Christ,
    who is one of us. Amen.

—Nancy S. Lapp, Goshen, Ind.

# Easter Season

## 45 Call to Worship

L: Christ is risen! Alleluia!
**P: Rejoice, O earth. Sing, O heavenly choirs.**
L: Give glory to God; our God has triumphed.
**P: God has become our strength and salvation.**
L: Christ, who was put to death on the cross,
    has been raised to life.
**P: Therefore, we shall not die, but we shall live
    and proclaim what the Lord has done.**
L: We have been raised to life with Christ
**P: and we know that when he appears,
    we shall appear with him and share his glory!**
L: This is the day of the Lord's victory.
**P: This is the day of the resurrection.
    Christ is risen. Alleluia!**

—Arlene M. Mark, in MPH Bulletin, 4-19-87 (adapted). Based on Ps. 118:14, 17;
    1 John 3:2

## 46 Call to Worship

L: This is the day which the Lord has made.
   Let us rejoice and be glad in it!

**P: This is the day the stone is cast aside,
   and the mantle of darkness is cast away!**

L: Be glad and rejoice—
   God has swallowed up death forever.

**P: This is the day of salvation.**

L: The Lord of light has come and reigns forever.
   Christ is risen!

**P: Christ is risen indeed!
   Alleluia! Amen.**

—Diane Karay, *All the Seasons of Mercy* (© 1987 Diane Karay; used by permission of Westminster John Knox Press), 62 (adapted). Based on Ps. 118:24; 1 Cor. 15:54

## 47 Prayer

God of terror and joy,
   you arise to shake the earth.
Open our inner graves
   so that all that has been buried
   may be freed and forgiven,
   and our lives may return to you
   through the risen Christ. Amen.

—Janet Morley, *All Desires Known* (Wilton, Conn.: Morehouse-Barlow, 1989), 16 (adapted). Based on Matt. 27:51-54, 28:1-10, Mark 16:1-8

## 48 Prayer

O Lord, your wondrous birth means nothing for us
   unless we are born again,
your sacrificial death means nothing for us
   unless we die to sin,
your triumphant resurrection means nothing for us

unless we be risen with you.
O Savior, raise and exalt us,
    now, to the estate of grace
    and hereafter to the state of glory;
where with the Father and the Holy Spirit
    you live and reign,
    God forever and ever. Amen.

—Eric Milner-White, *A Cambridge Bede Book* (London: Longmans, Green and Co., 1936), 15 (adapted)

## 49 Easter Prayer

O living God, who raised Jesus from the dead
    and brought new life on Easter morning,
    we lift our hearts in praise;
    we shout your great victory;
    we sing hymns of joy!
Even when our hearts are heavy
    and our eyes are dimmed by sorrow,
    you are ever faithful:
    you comfort all who mourn;
    you wipe away all tears;
    you bring joy in the morning.
Teach us, O God, to trust in your gracious love,
    to rest in your unfailing goodness,
    to hope in your true promise,
    that we may rejoice all our days
    and share the good news:
    death is defeated; all are made alive in you.
Alleluia! Amen.
Alleluia! Amen.

—Glenn W. Lehman, Leola, Pa., in MPH Bulletin, 3-26-89 (adapted)

## 50 Easter Prayer

Triumphant God,
>> we rejoice together
>> in the resurrection of Jesus Christ.
We give thanks for the faithful women
>> who traveled to the tomb early in the morning
>> and carried their fragrant spices.
We give thanks for the heavenly messenger
>> whose good news amazed the women
>> and transformed them into evangelists.
We give thanks for the glorious hope
>> that death has lost its sting
>> and joy comes forth from sorrow.
Renew your life in us, O God;
>> grant us courage to live
>> as people empowered by the resurrection
>> all the days of our lives!
We pray in the name of the risen Christ. Amen.

—Marlene Kropf, Elkhart, Ind., in MPH Bulletin, 3-31-91 (adapted). Based on Matt. 28:1-10

## 51 Prayer

God of holiness and light,
>> in the mystery of dying and rising with Christ,
>> you have established a new covenant of reconciliation.
Cleanse our hearts
>> and give a new spirit to all your people,
>> that your saving grace may be professed
>> and proclaimed to the whole world;
>> through Jesus Christ our Lord. Amen.

—*Liturgical Year,* Supplemental Liturgical Resource 7 (Louisville: Westminster John Knox Press, © 1992; used by permission of Westminster John Knox Press), 194

## 52  Easter Benediction

As Christ burst forth from the tomb,
　　may new life burst forth from us
　　and show itself in acts of love and healing
　　to a hurting world.
And may that same Christ,
　　who lives forever
　　and is the source of our new life,
　　keep your hearts rejoicing
　　and grant you peace this day and always. Amen.

—Carol A. Wise, in *For All Who Minister* (copyright © 1993, Brethren Press, Elgin, Ill.; used by permission)

## 53  Call to Worship for Ascension Day

L: Clap your hands, all you peoples;
　　shout to God with loud songs of joy.
**P: The Lord, the Most High, is awesome,**
　　**a great king over all the earth.**
L: The Lord is king, he is robed in majesty;
　　the Lord is robed, he is girded with strength.
**P: He has established the world,**
　　**it shall not be moved.**
L: Since, then, we have a great high priest
　　who has passed through the heavens,
　　Jesus, the Son of God,
　　let us hold fast to our confession.
**P: Let us approach the throne of grace with boldness,**
　　**so that we may receive mercy**
　　**and find grace to help in time of need.**

—Arlene M. Mark. Based on Pss. 47:1-2; 93:1-2; Heb. 4:14, 16

## 54 Prayer of Exaltation for Ascension Day

Almighty God,
    we thank you that you have highly exalted
    your Son, Jesus Christ.
Before him, every knee shall bow
    and every tongue confess
    that Jesus Christ is Lord.
He has made captivity itself a captive;
    and has given gifts to his people.
We rejoice that Jesus Christ,
    the pioneer and perfecter of our faith,
    has triumphed most gloriously
    and is our Lord.
Bring us, at last, into your presence,
    so that we can live and praise you
    together with all the saints
    forever and ever. Amen.

—Arlene M. Mark. Based on Phil. 2:5; Eph. 4:7; Heb. 12:1

# Pentecost Season

## 55 Call to Worship

L: Celebrate all nations;
    rejoice all peoples.
    The Holy Spirit has been poured out upon us.
**P: The fresh wind of the Spirit**
    **gives us thoughts above our thoughts.**
L: The discerning light of the Spirit
    shows us hidden recesses in our hearts.
**P: The unifying power of the Spirit**
    **kindles in us the fire of love.**

All: *As we worship,*
   *let the presence of the Spirit teach us,*
   *inspire us,*
   *and loosen our tongues in praise.*

—Arlene M. Mark

# 56  Pentecost Invocation

O brooding God,
   as your Spirit hovered over creation
      in fresh wind and new breath,
   so let your Spirit blow over us today
      with the breath of life.
   Take away the chaos of our lives,
      and the tiredness of our souls.
   May your Spirit move within us here today
      and then move us outward
         to proclaim our faith in word and deed. Amen.

—John William Lowe, Jr., in *Living Waters,* Worship Resources for
   Congregational Life 18, ed. by June A. Gibble (Elgin, Ill.: Church of the
   Brethren, Mar. 1994), 4 (adapted)

# 57  Invocations to the Spirit

God our Creator,
   our center, our friend,
**May the warm sun of your Spirit**
   **heal us this day.**
May the gentle rain of your Spirit
   refresh us this day.
**May the kindled fire of your Spirit**
   **blaze in us this day.**
May the fresh winds of your Spirit
   enliven us this day.

**May the dance of your Spirit**
**be our partner this day.**
**Amen.**

—Terry Falla, in *Be Our Freedom, Lord*, ed. by Terry Falla, 2d ed. (Adelaide: Open Book Publishers, 1994), 43

## 58 Prayer of Invitation

Come, Holy Spirit,
　　enter our lives,
　　whisper our names
　　and scatter your gifts of grace
　　with wild abandon.
　　Give your silent strength to all imprisoned
　　by the structures,
　　and let your raging fire be our sign of liberty.
Come, Holy Spirit,
　　help us find ourselves in vital places,
　　bringing your word of freedom
　　to the poor and the oppressed.

—Miriam T. Winter, *WomanWord* (New York: Crossword, 1990), 38 (adapted)

## 59 Prayer

Spirit of energy and change,
　　in whose power Jesus was anointed
　　　to be the hope of the nations;
　　pour yourself also upon us
　　　without reserve or distinction,
　　that we may have confidence and strength

> to plant justice and joy on the earth,
> through Jesus Christ. Amen.

—Janet Morley, *All Desires Known* (Wilton, Conn.: Morehouse-Barlow, 1989), 11
  (adapted)

# 60  Pentecost Benediction

Given power by the Spirit,
>   let us go into the world,
>     bringing understanding to those living in despair
>     and freshness of life to those living in death. Amen.

—John William Lowe, Jr., in *Living Waters*, Worship Resources for
  Congregational Life 18, ed. by June A. Gibble (Elgin, Ill.: Church of the
  Brethren, Mar. 1994), 4 (adapted)

# 61  Call to Worship for Trinity Sunday

L: Let us worship in the name of the Father.
**P: Salvation and glory and power to our God,**
>     **for the Lord our God the Almighty reigns.**

L: Let us worship in the name of the Son,
**P: who gave himself for our sins**
>     **to set us free from this evil age,**
>     **according to the will of the Father.**

L: Let us worship in the name of the Holy Spirit,
**P: for all who are led by the Spirit**
>     **are children of God.**

> All: **The grace of the Lord Jesus Christ,**
> **the love of God,**
> **and the communion of the Holy Spirit**
> **are with us here**
> **to fill our hearts**
> **and change our lives.**

—Arlene M. Mark. Based on Rev. 19; Gal. 1:3; Rom. 8:14; 2 Cor. 13:13

# 62 All Saints' Day Prayer

*(November 1 or first Sunday in November)*

L: It is right and good to give you thanks, Almighty God,
for you are the source of light and life.

P: **You made us in your image**
**and called us to new life in Jesus Christ.**

L: In all times and places
your people proclaim your glory in unending praise.

P: **We praise you today for saints and martyrs,**
**faithful people in every age**
**who have followed your Son, Jesus Christ.**

L: As they witnessed to Christ's resurrection,
may we be strengthened by their witness
and supported by their fellowship,

P: **that we may run with perseverance**
**the race that lies before us**
**and with them, receive the unfading crown of glory.**
**We praise you, almighty God,**
**through Christ, your Son in the Holy Spirit. Amen.**

—Lombard (Ill.) Mennonite Church Bulletin, 11-1-87. Based on Heb. 11:1—12:3;
1 Pet. 5:4

## 63  All Saints' Day Prayer

O Lord our God, we bless you
>    for the glorious company of apostles,
>    the goodly fellowship of the prophets,
>    the noble army of martyrs,
>    and all who have served faithfully
>    in your church throughout the world.

We bless you for those who by their speech,
>    their writing, and their lives
>    have enabled us to see more of your glory.

We bless you for all who have helped and comforted,
>    strengthened and encouraged us on our way.

For all whom you have called to be saints,
>    through whom you have made manifest
>    the riches of your grace,
>    we praise you, O God.

We ask that with them, and with all the host of the redeemed,
>    we may perfectly praise you in your heavenly kingdom,
>    through Jesus Christ our Lord. Amen.

—J. M. Todd, *Prayers and Services for Christian Festivals* (London: Oxford Univ.
Press, Amen House, 1951), 71-72 (adapted). Based on Heb. 11:1—12:3

## 64  Prayer for Christ the King Sunday

*(The Sunday preceding Advent)*

High King of Heaven, accept our adoration
>    even as you are adored by angels around your throne
>    and by Jesus Christ, the firstborn of the dead.

We praise you that Christ has redeemed us
>    and made us to be a kingdom, priests to serve you, O God.

Grant us courage to live sacrificial lives,
>    dedicated to unlimited and unending service,
>    even as Christ came to serve and not to be served.

Grant us boldness to answer your call to discipleship
    and willingness to follow Christ's example
    that your work may be done and your kingdom come
    through Jesus Christ,
    to whom be glory and dominion forever and ever. Amen.

—Arlene M. Mark. Based on Rev. 1:4-6; 4:6-8; 5:10; 6:9-11; Mark 10:45

# Other Special Times

## New Year

### 65 New Year's Prayer

L: Hear my prayer, O Lord,
    let my cry come before you.

**P: My days pass away like smoke,**
    **my heart withers like grass.**

L: But you, O Lord, are enthroned forever,
    you are ageless throughout all generations.

**P: Long ago you laid the foundations of the earth,**
    **and the heavens are the work of your hands.**

L: They will perish, but you will endure;

**P: they will all wear out like a garment.**

L: You change them like clothing, and they pass away;

**P: but you are the same, and your years have no end.**

L: Happy are those whose hope is in the Lord their God
    who made heaven and earth, and all that is in them;
    who keeps faith forever.

**P: Because you, O God, are our past, our present, our future,**
    **the same now and always,**
    **we will serve and bless you. Amen.**

—Arlene M. Mark. Based on Pss. 29:10; 102:25-28; 146:1

## 66 New Year's Prayer

Immortal God,
you are from everlasting to everlasting;
    with you there is no beginning or end.
You oversee the endlessness of space,
    yet each of us is always in your view.
You are always creating, all things become new,
    yet you abide the same forever.
We begin this New Year,
    confident in your keeping power,
    assured of your infinity.
May we mirror your virtue,
    model your suffering love,
    live your righteousness.
By your grace, enable us to serve you,
    to worship and glorify you,
    through Jesus Christ, our Lord. Amen.

—Arlene M. Mark. Based on Pss. 90; 104; Rev. 21:5

## 67 New Year's Prayer

Almighty God,
    who makest all things new
    and abidest forever the same,
encourage us to reach forward
    and to set our hope upon your promises;
so that, going on into the New Year with trustful hearts,
    we may be able in all that we do
    to please your loving eyes;
    through Jesus Christ our Lord. Amen.

—*Mozarabic Sacramentary* (Spain, ca. 6th century); in *Book of Worship* (Elgin, Ill.: Brethren Press, 1964), 168 (adapted; prayer copyright holder unknown)

## 68 New Year's Prayer

L: As our year changes, we come to you, O God.

**P: You, O God, are from everlasting to everlasting.**
   **You do not change. Your steadfast love is our stability.**

L: We stop and consider as we begin this New Year.

**P: There are old fears but new boldness;**
   **there are old controversies but new options;**
   **there are old problems but new potential.**

L: You are a God of hope; show us new dreams.

**P: You are a God of promise; show us new possibilities.**

L: How great is your wisdom and knowledge.
   Your ways are beyond our comprehension. Teach us.

**P: Your Word is full of wisdom.**
   **Your Spirit moves among us in unexpected ways.**
   **Teach us to think your thoughts, O God,**
      **for to understand you is better than offering gold,**
      **and to follow your way is better than bringing jewels.**

L: As we join the seekers for the Christ Child,
   lead us by the light of Christ's teachings.

**P: Show us the way; guide us by your light.**
   **We bow down to worship you;**
   **we bring our lives as gifts of praise to you.**

*All: We pray in the name of the one who led the wise men*
   *and still leads those who seek him. Amen.*

—Arlene M. Mark. Based on Pss. 90:2; 139:6

# Thanksgiving Day, Labor Day

## 69 Thanksgiving Call to Worship

1: Ascribe to the Lord the glory due his name;
   bring an offering, and come before him.

2: Worship the Lord in holy splendor;
   tremble before him, all the earth.

1: The earth has yielded its increase;
   God, our God, has blessed us.

2: May God continue to bless us;
   let all the ends of the earth revere God.

—Arlene M. Mark. Based on 1 Chron. 16:29; Ps. 67:6-7

## 70 Thanksgiving Call to Worship

L: Give thanks to the Lord, proclaim God's greatness.

**P: Tell the nations what God has done.**

L: Sing praise to the Lord.

**P: Tell the wonderful things God has done.**

L: Be glad that we belong to God.

**P: Let all who worship God rejoice.**

L: The Lord is our God; God's commands are for all the world.

**P: God will keep his covenant forever,**
**God's promises last for a thousand generations.**
**Praise the Lord!**

—Arlene M. Mark. Based on Ps. 105, GNB

## 71 Thanksgiving Readings

L: Give thanks to God, for God is good.

**P: God has set the earth firmly on its foundations,**
**and it will never be moved.**

L: God placed the ocean over it like a robe, and the waters flow
over the mountains and into the valleys.

**P: God created the moon to tell the months,**
**and the sun to mark the days.**

L: God has made so many things!
In wisdom God made them all.

**P: Give thanks to God for God is good.**

\* \* \*

L: Give thanks to God for God is good.

**P: Great is God's love, higher than the heavens.**
**God's faithfulness reaches to the skies.**

L: God has made known to me the path of life;
God's presence gives me unbounded joy.

**P: My future is in God's hand;**
**God is near, and nothing can shake me.**

L: I am thankful and glad, for I feel completely secure.

**P: Give thanks to God, for God is good.**

\* \* \*

L:  Give thanks to God, for God is good.
**P:  When we were overwhelmed by sin,**
    **God atoned for our transgressions.**
L:  God lifted me from the pit of sin
    and set me safely on a rock.
**P:  God made me a new creation**
    **and gave me a new song to sing.**
L:  Thanks be to God for his priceless gift,
    even his Son, our Savior.
**P:  Give thanks to God, for God is good.**

—Arlene M. Mark. Based on Pss. 104; 108; 107; 40:2-4; 2 Cor. 9:15 (GNB)

# 72  Prayer of Thanksgiving

Gracious God,
your heart abounds with goodness,
    and your hand pours out abundance.
We praise you for the continuous cycle
    of seedtime and harvest
    and the order of nature.
We bless you for the beauty of autumn
    and its generous yield.
We thank you that you are mindful of us
    and supply our needs.
Accept our thanksgiving and our praise
    for the cycle of life
    and for all the joys of living. Amen.

—Arlene M. Mark

# 73 Prayer of Thanksgiving

We thank you, God,
> for this amazing day;
> for the true dream of a cloud-filled sky,
> for the cool embrace of a comforting breeze,
> for everything that is natural,
>> which is infinite, which is alive,
>> which is a part of your dynamic creation.

We thank you, God,
> for the phenomenon which we know as life.

We experience life
> as joy at the birth of a child,
> as love when we find others who share with us,
> as exhilaration of victory in sporting events,
>> academic debate, business ventures,
> as fulfilling satisfaction when we achieve,
> as confusion and disappointment when others fail us,
> as anxiety and pain when illness intervenes,
> as fear and hurt when death takes someone we love.

We acknowledge the complex rhythms of nature
> that make life different for each of us,

but we are brought together by a community of faith
> which interweaves us to one another,
> individuals bound by common purpose
> and circle of concern.

We give thanks for this spirit of humanity.

In all we do and experience, O God,
> teach us first to love, for love is most precious.

Love knows no limit to its endurance,
> no end to its trust, no fading of its hope.

It outlasts anything, and it stands when all else has fallen.

When we love, it is easier to speak;
> it is easier to listen;
> it is easier to play;
> it is easier to work;
> it is easier to cry;
> it is easier to laugh.

Teach us that love is the truest of all seasons;
>give us desire and willingness to share its beauty.
Teach us that of all the music of this earth,
>that which reaches the farthest into heaven
>is the beating of a loving heart.
Now, O God, in the silence of this moment,
>we pray for a reawakening of our senses to this day.
Open our minds to all that is ours—
>to imagination, to understanding,
>to a sense of peace, to constant singing.
And when this day is done,
>give us hope for another day,
>to experience your enduring love.
For all that we are, this is our prayer. Amen.

—E. LaVern Epp, Lawrence, Kan. (adapted). Written at the death of his father. Based on 1 Cor. 13

## 74 Thanks for Fun Times

L: Thank you, God, for sunny days,
>for my favorite colors,
>and dogs with wagging tails.
**P: Thank you, God, for trees to climb,**
>**and cubbyholes to hide in,**
>**for parks with slides and swings.**
L: Thank you, God, for my rubber boots
>and my rain coat, for puddles
>to splash in, and leaves to kick.
**P: Thank you God, for beach balls**
>**and surfboards, for warm sand**
>**and the cool sea to swim in.**
*All: Thank you, God, for friends to play with,*
>*and for everyone who loves me very much.*
>*Thank you God, for me.*

—Daniel, Jeremy, Matthew, and Terry Falla, in *Be Our Freedom, Lord*, ed. by Terry Falla (Adelaide: Lutheran Publishing House, 1984), 76

## 75 Litany of Thanksgiving

L: Gracious God,
    you supply us with blessings beyond our deserving.
  We thank you for your creation,
    and every sign of your presence within it,
    for your everlasting grace and forgiveness,
    for the risen Lord who has gone before us
    and calls us to follow him.

**P: Accept our thanks, O God.**

L: For our homes and our loved ones,
    for work to do and strength to do it,
    for moments of gladness that sparkle our day,

**P: accept our thanks, O God.**

L: For our faith and all that sustains it,
    for all whose lives and examples have persuaded us
    that the journey is worth the taking,
    for your caring discipline that keeps our faith pure,

**P: accept our thanks, O God.**

L: For the depths of the sea where our falseness lies buried,
    for the guiding comfort of your Holy Spirit,
    for the powerful promise of life everlasting,

**P: accept our thanks, O God,**
   **for yours is the glory forever. Amen.**

—Arlene M. Mark

## 76 Prayer About Work for Labor Day

Creating God, source of energy and power,
  Maker of the universe, we bless you.
You established for us rhythms of work and rest.
  Help us to realize that we cannot improve on your pattern.
  Give us the creativity and freedom
  to discover our individual variations.
Jesus, our model and master,
  was known as the son of a carpenter,
  who lived, loved, worked, and rested, even as do we.
Teach us the balance

that neither glorifies nor demeans physical labor,
  that values people because they are your creation.
Let us neither idolize the work of our intellect and skills,
  nor excuse ourselves for doing less than our best.
In the name of the Lord Jesus, we offer to you, our God,
  all we do in word or deed, giving thanks for your gifts
  of life, health, and strength,
  without which we can do nothing.
This hour of this morning we put aside our labors
  and dedicate our hearts and minds in worshiping you,
  great Creator God. Amen.

—E. Elaine Kauffman, Elkhart, Ind. Based on Col. 3:17; Matt. 13:55

# Missions

## 77 Mission Sunday Call to Worship

L: Sing to the Lord, all the earth.
    Tell of his salvation from day to day.
**P: Declare his glory among the nations,**
    **his marvelous works among all the peoples.**
L: For great is the Lord, and greatly to be praised;
    God is to be revered above all gods.
**P: For all the gods of the peoples are idols,**
    **but the Lord made the heavens.**
*All: Honor and majesty are before him,*
    *strength and joy are in his place.*

—1 Chron. 16:23-25

## 78 Praise for Missions

L: The God who made the world
    and everything in it
    is Lord of heaven and earth
    and gives to mortals life and breath.

All who search for God will find him,
for he is not far from us.

**P:  Thanks be to God**
**for the revelation of himself**
**as God of all peoples.**

L:  Many shall come from the east and the west
and will sit down in the kingdom of heaven.

**P:  Thanks be to God**
**for the gift of salvation**
**for all peoples.**

L:  Jesus announced:
"The kingdom of God has come near;
repent, and believe in the good news."
"As the Father has sent me,
so I send you."

**P:  Having received this command,**
**let us witness to the gospel;**
**it is the power of God for salvation**
**to everyone who has faith.**

L:  The mission of the church
is to make disciples of all nations,
baptizing them and teaching them
by word and witness that Jesus is Lord.

*All:  We believe that life can find fulfillment*
*nowhere except in Christ.*
*Let us proclaim the message of deliverance*
*and live as faithful followers*
*of Jesus Christ until he comes.*

—Arlene M. Mark. Based on Acts 17:24, 27; Matt. 8:11, Mark 1:15, John 20·21;
Rom. 1:16; Matt. 28:18-20

# 79  Missions Prayer

O Lord our God,
listening to us in this place
you accept also the prayers of our sisters and brothers
in Africa, Asia, Australia, America, and Europe.
We are all one in prayer.

So may we, as one, rightly carry out your commission
 to witness and to live
 in the church and throughout the world.
Accept all our prayers graciously,
 those in our words and those in strange languages.
 They are offered in Jesus' name. Amen.

—From the Ghanaian Church, in *The Iona Community Worship Book* (Glasgow: Wild Goose Pubns., 1987), 97c (adapted)

# 80   Prayer

O Lord God,
 who has called us your servants to ventures
 of which we cannot see the ending,
 by paths as yet untrodden,
 through perils unknown:
Give us faith to go out with good courage,
 not knowing where we go,
 but only that your hand is leading us
 and your love supporting us;
 through Jesus Christ our Lord. Amen.

—From *Lutheran Book of Worship* (copyright © 1978, by permission of Augsburg Fortress, may not be reproduced without permission of Augsburg Fortress)

# Peace and Justice

## 81   Peace Sunday Call to Worship

L: Let us gather with the faithful
 from every nation, race, people, and language,
 to worship the God made known to us in Christ Jesus.

**P: To God, the ruler of the universe, and to Jesus the Lamb
 be blessing and honor, glory and might forever and ever.**

L: Let us gather in God's presence,
 singing songs of praise and joy,
 with the people of God in every place and time.

P: **Holy, holy, holy,**
    **great God of Hosts!**
**The whole earth is full of God's glory.**
**Glory be to God most high.**

—Ruth C Duck, *Flames of the Spirit* (Cleveland· Pilgrim Press, 1985), 58
(adapted). Based on Rev. 7:9, 12, 4:8, 5:12, Isa. 6:3

# 82 Prayer for Unity

O loving, sovereign God,
    whose reign extends round our globe and beyond,
    we rejoice in your far-flung greatness;
    we give thanks for your unending goodness.
In all the corners of the earth,
you are faithfully building your church:
    in crowded Indian villages,
    in sunny Caribbean islands,
    in remote Chinese hamlets,
    in busy South African townships,
    in racially diverse North American cities.
We give thanks for the vast embrace of your love,
    for the multicolored church you are creating.
Grant, O God, that we may truly be one church
    with one baptism, one hope, in one Lord Jesus Christ,
    to the end of the age, to the praise of God's glory. Amen.

—Marlene Kropf, Elkhart, Ind., in MPH Bulletin, 5-7-89. Based on John 17·21-23

# 83 Prayer for Peacemaking

O God,
    by your Son Jesus Christ,
    you have broken down the walls of partition
    between Jew and Gentile, slave and free,
    rich and poor, male and female.
Break down all the barriers that divide us;
    remove the hindrances that keep us apart.

Reveal our jealousies and show us our pride;
>cure our alienation;
>open up our narrowness.
Shatter all prejudice
>though we may have different histories,
>different cultures, different viewpoints.
May we live together as loving neighbors,
>in honor preferring one another,
>to the glory of your great name. Amen.

—Arlene M. Mark. Based on Col. 3:11; Eph. 2:14

# 84  Call to Worship

L:  The Lord of hosts is with us;
>the God of Jacob is our refuge.
>Come, behold the works of the Lord.
**P:  God makes wars to cease to the end of the earth;**
>**God breaks the bow, and shatters the spear,**
>**and burns the chariots with fire!**
L:  Be still, and know that God is God.
>God is exalted among the nations, and exalted in the earth!
**P:  The Lord of hosts is with us;**
>**The God of Jacob is our refuge.**

—Margaret Richer Smith, Lombard, Ill. Based on Ps. 46:7-11

# 85  World Family Reading

L:  O for a world where everyone
>respects each other's ways,
**P:  where love is lived and all is done**
>**with justice and with praise.**
L:  O for a world where goods are shared
>and misery relieved,

P: **where truth is spoken, children spared,**
> **equality achieved.**

L: We welcome one world family
> and struggle with each choice
> that opens us to unity
> and gives our vision voice.

P: **The poor are rich, the weak are strong,**
> **the foolish ones are wise.**
> **Tell all who mourn, outcasts belong,**
> **who perishes will rise.**

All: *O for a world preparing for*
> *God's glorious reign of peace,*
> *where time and tears will be no more,*
> *and all but love will cease.*

—Miriam T. Winter, *WomanWord* (New York: Crossroad, 1990), 318 (adapted)

# 86 Prayer for Peace

In these our days so perilous,
> Lord, peace in mercy send us.
No God but thee can fight for us,
> no God but thee defend us.
Thou our only God and Savior.

—Martin Luther, *Hymns* (1529); reprinted from *Prayers of the Reformers*, ed. by Clyde Manschreck (© 1958 Muhlenberg Press; used by permission of Augsburg Fortress; may not be reproduced without permission of Augsburg Fortress), 49, no. 13

# 87 Litany for Peace and Justice

L: O God, the heavens are yours and the earth is yours.
> All our life belongs to you.

P: **Make us your messengers of peace and justice.**

L: May your kingdom come and your will be done on earth,
    as it is in heaven.

**P: Make us your messengers of peace and justice.**

L: May all injustice, violence, and oppression give way
    to fairness, mercy, and good will.

**P: Make us your messengers of peace and justice.**

L: Teach us to use the manifold resources of the earth
    so that none may waste and none may want.

**P: Make us your messengers of peace and justice.**

L: In all our labors, may cooperation triumph over conflict;
    may all people find their reward
    in work that serves the good of all.

**P: Make us your messengers of peace and justice.**

L: Keep alive the holy fire within the hearts
    of all who dare to be the voices of unwelcome wisdom.
    Make us willing to hear hard demands.

**P: Make us your messengers of peace and justice.**

L: Fill us with a passion for righteousness
    and a zeal to serve where there is need.
    Fill us with a purpose that is holy and right and just.
    Help us to love the noblest and best.

**P: Make us your messengers of peace and justice.**

*All: Unto you, O God, be all might and majesty,*
        *dominion and power, both now and evermore. Amen.*

—Adapted from *Lift Up Your Hearts* by Walter Russell Bowie (copyright renewal © 1984 by Mrs. Jean B. Evans, Mrs. Elizabeth Chapman, and Mrs. Walter Russell Bowie, Jr.; used by permission of the publisher, Abingdon Press)

# Mutual Aid, Stewardship, School

## 88 Reading for Mutual Aid

L: Great is the Lord, and greatly to be praised.
    The Lord is good to all
        and has compassion on all that has been made.

P: **Happy are those who fear the Lord,**
   **who find great delight in God's commandments.**
   **They rise in the darkness as a light for the upright;**
   **they are gracious, compassionate, and righteous.**
   **Good will come to those who are generous and lend freely;**
   **who conduct their affairs with justice.**

L: For the righteous will never be moved;
   they will be remembered forever.
   They have distributed freely; they have given to the poor.

All: *All the faithful will bless God's name;*
   *to all peoples they will make known God's mighty deeds*
   *and the glorious splendor of God's kingdom.*

—MMA, *Mutual Aid Worship Res.*, 6 (1994; adapted). Based on Pss. 112; 145

# 89 Commitment to Caring

L: Give thanks in all circumstances;
   for this is the will of God in Christ Jesus for you.

P: **Be on guard against all greed, for one's life does not consist**
   **in the abundance of possessions.**

L: Bear one another's burdens,
   and in this way you will fulfill the law of Christ.

P: **None should seek their own good, but the good of others.**

L: Whoever does not provide for relatives,
   and especially for family members,
   has denied the faith and is worse than an unbeliever.

P: **Contribute to the needs of the saints;**
   **extend hospitality to strangers.**

All: *By our work we must support the weak,*
   *remembering the words of the Lord Jesus:*
   *"It is more blessed to give than to receive."*

—David E. Hostetler, Scottdale, Pa., in MPH Bulletin, 9-17-89 (adapted). Based on 1 Thess. 4:18; Luke 12:15; Gal. 6:2; 1 Cor. 10:24; 1 Tim. 5:8; Rom. 12:13; Acts 20:34-35

# 90 Prayer

O Lord, who though you were rich,
 yet for our sakes did become poor,
 you have promised in your gospel
 that whatsoever is done unto the least,
 you will receive as done unto you.
Give us grace, we humbly beseech you,
 to be ever willing and ready to minister, as you enable us,
 to the necessities of our brothers and sisters,
 and to extend the blessings of your kingdom
 over all the world, to your praise and glory,
 who are God over all, blessed forever. Amen.

—Augustine of Hippo (A.D. 354-430), in MPH Bulletin, 9-18-88

# 91 A Stewardship Covenant

L: The earth is the Lord's and everything in it.

**P: We pledge to care for God's creation
so that it will nourish and beautify the lives of all.**

L: All humanity is God's creation.

**P: We pledge to live in unity and fellowship
so that all peoples can reflect God's goodness.**

L: God has given us wisdom and sound minds.

**P: We pledge to yield them to God's guidance
so that we can receive God's instruction.**

L: God has given us the liberty of moral choice.

**P: We pledge to make decisions considerately
so that our judgments will be wise and fair.**

L: God has given us the Word as directive for living.

**P: We pledge to establish it in our hearts
so that we can live in meaningful obedience.**

L: From each to whom much has been given, much is required.

P: **We pledge to give freely of all that we have received
so that God's generous gifts be shared fairly and
God's name be honored in all the earth, world without end.**

—Arlene M. Mark, MPH Bulletin, 11-14-82. Based on Pss. 24:1, 8, 1 2, Luke
12:48

# 92 Prayer for Heritage Sunday

God of all ages,
we thank you for the heritage
which is the foundation of our faith.
We affirm the faith we have received
and those who nurtured us along the way.
We thank you for the faithful prayers of our mothers
and the caring examples of our fathers.
We thank you for those heroes of faith
who have gone before,
living by their beliefs
and dying for their convictions.
We thank you for our everyday models of uprightness,
who guide us into truth
by forthright witness and gentle affirmation.
We thank you for those who found loyalty costly
and those who are devout in the midst of ease.
May we walk worthily of those
in whose unseen presence we live.
Save us from cowardly surrender to the world,
that the faith we proclaim will be strong and true,
boldly affirming your return
to receive the faithful unto yourself
for all eternity. Amen.

—Arlene M. Mark

## 93   Prayer for Acceptance of All

Tender and compassionate God,
we thank you for inviting all your children
    into your kingdom.
Let us see each other with your eyes.
Too often we are afraid
    to examine ways we fall short of your kingdom purpose
    for our lives as individuals and as a community;
    to accept without reservation
        those who are disabled in body or mind.
Forgive our apathy, our narrow-mindedness,
    our misunderstandings.
Forgive our laziness of effort to be inclusive,
    to love spontaneously,
    to welcome genuinely.
Call forth our best selves,
    and help us lift each other up.
Bless those among us with disabilities,
    those who are still outside looking in,
    those who long to feel included.
Prepare our hearts to set about the work
    of being one people,
    the inclusive body of Christ,
    ministers of unconditional love.
May we follow the example of Christ,
    who opened himself to all,
    the powerful and powerless alike.
Through his name, we pray. Amen.

—Arlene M. Mark. Based on an MCC Disability Awareness Prayer

# 94 Prayer for Church School Day

God of all wisdom,
> you formed us in your image.
In your likeness we think and move and have our being.
You have given us the gift of thought
> that we might understand your handiwork with reverence.
We praise you, O Lord,
> that your Spirit inspires understanding,
for without it we have no discernment
> to separate truth from error.
May our minds be servants, governed by your will,
> and not idols for our own selfish goals.

We thank you for our Christian schools,
> where we learn about your great creation
> and about you as Creator.
For those who pioneered with vision and courage
> and those who continue to nurture Christian values,
> we give you praise.
May we join with them in the serious task
> of building up the body of Christ.

Enlighten us with your wisdom
> so that the truth that makes us free
> will direct us in serving you
> from generation to generation. Amen.

—Arlene M. Mark. Based on John 8:32

# All Seasons

## Gathering, Calls to Worship

### 95 Call to Worship

L: Come, people of God, and worship the Christ.
Once we were separated from him,
aliens and strangers who did not belong,
without hope and without God in the world.
Once we loved darkness rather than light.
Once we could not sing the Lord's song.

**P: But now we are joined with Christ,**
**brought near through his blood,**
**for He is our peace.**
**Now we who lived in darkness**
**have come into the light.**
**Now we who could not sing**
**have been given a new song.**

*All: Let us give thanks to God!*
*Let us worship the Christ!*

—Marlene Kropf, Elkhart, Ind. Based on Eph. 2:12-13; John 3:19; Ps. 137

## 96 Call to Worship

L: Come, let us worship and bow down.
    Let us kneel before the Lord our Maker!

**P: The Lord is a great God,
and a great King above all gods.**

L: Let us extol God in the congregation of the people;
    let us praise God in our assembly.

**P: Great is the Lord, and greatly to be praised;
God's greatness is unsearchable.**

L: Ascribe to the Lord glory and strength;
    worship the Lord in holy splendor.

**P: Holy, holy, holy is the Lord of hosts.
The whole earth is full of God's glory.**

—Arlene M. Mark. Based on Pss. 95:6, 3; 7:32; 145:3; 29:1-2; Isa. 6:3

## 97 Call to Worship

L: The Lord is in his holy temple;
    let all the earth be silent before him.

**P: God is here among us and within us.
We await God's word.**

L: God's greatness fills us
    with wonder and with awe.

**P: Holy, holy, holy is the Lord of hosts;
the whole earth is full of his glory.**

*All: We worship a holy God,
who inhabits our world
and lives within us.*

—Arlene M. Mark, in *Worship Resources* (Worship Series), ed. by Arlene M. Mark (MPH, 1982), 30. Based on Hab. 2:20; Isa. 6

## 98  Call to Worship

*(correlate with no. 133)*

L: Praise the Lord,
    who does not hide
    when we seek his face.

**P: Praise the Lord,**
    **who hears our cry**
    **and answers when we call.**

L: The Lord does not turn away in anger
    but helps us in our distress.

**P: The Lord our God and Savior**
    **never rejects or forsakes us.**

L: The Lord protects us from oppressors
    who threaten us with lies and violence.

*All: We walk in confidence;*
    *our Lord is strong.*

—Ferne Burkhardt, Petersburg, Ont., in MPH Bulletin, 9-29-91 (adapted). Based on Ps. 27:8

## 99  Preparation for Gathering

As God's people, we have gathered.
We may be discouraged,
    dismayed, discordant with life.
Let us sit together,
    sharing the solace of silence.
Let us possess the peace of God's presence
    and be wrapped in the warmth of God's love.
Let us be comforted and quieted,
    prepared for communion with God
    and fellowship with one another.

—Arlene M. Mark

## 100 Call to Worship

L: Open to us the gates of righteousness!

**P: We will enter through them and give thanks to the Lord.**

L: This is the gate of the Lord;
only the righteous shall enter through it.

**P: We will give thanks to the Lord;
God has become our salvation.**

L: The stone that the builders rejected
has become the chief cornerstone.

**P: This is the Lord's doing;
it is marvelous in our eyes.**

L: O give thanks to the Lord, for the Lord is good.
God's steadfast love endures forever.

**P: This is the day that the Lord has made;
let us rejoice and be glad.**

—Marlene Kropf, Elkhart, Ind. Based on Ps. 118:19-27; 1 Pet. 2:7

## 101 Gathering Words

We have gathered as God's people
to delight in God's presence,
to experience God's healing,
to receive God's grace.
Let us be reconciled and renewed
as we worship our God
through Christ
in the Spirit.

—Arlene M. Mark

## 102 Call to Worship
*(correlate with no. 127)*

L: Let us receive the message of God,
   which I have heard and declare unto you.
P: **God is love; every one that loves
   is born of God and knows God.**
L: God is light; in God is not darkness at all.
   When we walk in the light,
      we have fellowship with one another.
P: **Let us declare the praises of God,
   who called us out of darkness
      into this wonderful light
      and this fellowship of love.**

—Arlene M. Mark. Based on 1 John 1:5; 3:11; 1 Pet. 2:9

## 103 Call to Worship

L: Grace and peace to you this day
      from God the Father
      and the Lord Jesus Christ.
P: **Blessed be the Father of our Lord Jesus Christ,
      who has blessed us in Christ with every spiritual blessing.**
L: Before the world was made, God chose us in Christ
      to be holy and blameless before him in love.
P: **According to God's great pleasure,
      we are adopted as God's children,
      redeemed according to God's good pleasure.**
L: In Christ we have redemption through his blood,
      the forgiveness of sins,
      according to the riches of his grace.

> All: **For this reason we bow before the Father.**
> **To him be glory in the church and in Christ Jesus**
> **to all generations, forever and ever.**

—Arlene M. Mark. Based on Eph. 1; 3

# 104 Call to Worship

L: Glorify the Lord with me;
let us exalt God's name together.
**P: We will bless the Lord at all times;**
**God's praise will always be on our lips.**
L: When we wander afar, God welcomes us back.
**P: When we cry out in despair,**
**God hears and delivers us**
**from all our troubles.**
L: Taste and see that the Lord is good.
**P: Happy are we when we take refuge in God's care.**

—Arlene M. Mark, in MPH Bulletin, 3-29-92. Based on Ps. 34, NIV

# 105 Call to Worship

L: We come together as the family of faith.
**P: We assemble to honor the living God.**
L: Through Christ we become God's holy household.
**P: In Christ we are bonded together to be God's people.**
L: Our worship is united into oneness by the Holy Spirit.
**P: In communion with the Holy Spirit,**
**let us celebrate our unity.**

—Arlene M. Mark, in *Worship Resources* (Worship Series), ed. by Arlene M. Mark
(MPH, 1982), 31

## 106 A General Blessing

L: God has breathed the breath of life within you.

**P: Blessed be God, and God's blessing be upon us.**

L: God has saved us from sin and death through grace.

**P: Blessed be God, and God's blessing be upon us.**

L: God has empowered us to serve others in Christ's name.

**P: Blessed be God, and God's blessing be upon us.**

—Vienna Cobb Anderson, *Prayers of Our Hearts: In Word and Action* (New York: Crossroad, 1991), 216 (adapted)

## 107 Call to Worship

L: Come, worship the Christ, a living stone,
　　rejected by mortals but precious in God's sight.

**P: We are like living stones
　　being used in building the spiritual temple,
　　with Christ as our cornerstone.**

L: We will offer spiritual sacrifices
　　acceptable to God through Jesus Christ,

**P: for we are a chosen people, a royal priesthood,
　　a holy nation, God's own people.**

L: Once we were no people,
　　but now we are God's people.

**P: Therefore, we declare the mighty acts of God,
　　who calls us out of darkness into his marvelous light.
　　We will be priests of good news
　　and serve each other,
　　with Christ as our example.**

—Arlene M. Mark. Based on 1 Pet. 2:2-10, 21-25

# 108 Call to Worship

L: Let us worship the eternal God,
  the Source of love and life,
  who creates us.

**P: Let us worship Jesus Christ,**
  **the risen one, who lives among us.**

L: Let us worship the Spirit,
  the Holy Fire, who renews us.

*All: To the one true God be praise*
  *in all times and places,*
  *through the grace of Jesus Christ.*

—Ruth C. Duck, in *Touch Holiness*, ed. by Ruth C. Duck and Maren C. Tirabassi (Cleveland: Pilgrim Press, 1990), 93

# 109 Call to Worship

L: Holy, holy, holy is the Lord.
  The Lord is holy in all his ways.

**P: God is holy, enthroned on the praises of his people.**
  **Praise the Lord our God; holy is he.**

L: God has called us with a holy calling,
  to be holy and blameless before him in love,
 not because of what we have done,
  but because of his own purpose and grace.

**P: As God who called us is holy,**
  **we ourselves must be holy in all conduct,**
 **for it is written, "You shall be holy, for I am holy."**

*All: Holy, holy, holy, the Lord God the Almighty,*
  *who was and is and is to come.*

—Arlene M. Mark. Based on Pss. 145:17; 22:3; 99:5; 2 Tim. 1:9; Eph. 1:4; 1 Pet. 1:2; Rev. 4:8

## 110 Call to Worship

    L:  In holy splendor, we worship the Lord.

    **P:  In God is glory and strength.**

*All:  The Lord is mighty. God is with us.*

    L:  In torrents and storms, God's peace pervades.

    **P:  In rumbling thunder, the mighty voice soothes.**

*All:  The Lord is majestic. God is with us.*

    L:  The whisper of the Lord snaps silence.

    **P:  The unwavering sound persists.**

*All:  The Lord is awesome. God is with us.*

    L:  As flames being fanned, the presence grows.

    **P:  In its shadow the wilderness pleads.**

*All:  The Lord is powerful. God is with us.*

    L:  Enthroned, God rules the universe.

    **P:  The peaceful scepter prevails.**

*All:  God reigns. God is with us.*

    L:  In whirling winds, nature acknowledges glory.

    **P:  The people in the temple rejoice.**

*All:  It is certain. God is with us.*

—Lara J. Hall, Scottdale, Pa. Based on Ps. 29

## 111 Call to Worship

*(correlate with no. 134)*

9-25-13

*All:  This is the day the Lord has made.*
     *Let us rejoice and be glad in it.*

L: Again today we come together to worship—
     the God of creation, of salvation,
     of time and eternity.
    The God of all peoples, of all nations,
     of all conditions of people everywhere.

*All:  Praise the Lord.*
     *All that is within me,*
      *praise God's holy name.*

L: Praise the Lord and remember all his kindness:
in forgiving our sins;
in curing our diseases;
in saving us from destruction;
in surrounding us with love.

*All: The Lord is full of mercy and compassion.*
*The Lord is slow to anger*
*and willing to give us gifts of love.*
*Praise the Lord!*
*Oh, praise the Lord, all that is within me.*

—Roy Umble, Goshen, Ind. Based on Pss. 118:24; 103

# 112 Call to Worship

L: We come together as the church of Jesus Christ,
recognizing that our Lord lived and died,
not just for the church, but for all people,
God's highest creation.

**P: For God so loved the world that he gave his only Son.**

L: We also recognize that in God's great love,
we sense our need first to be loved
and thus to be turned around,
to face the needs of others.

**P: We love, because God first loved us.**

L: Let us love, then, so that we may be free of selfish desires,
liberated to strive for God's will.

**P: Whatever we do to the least of God's family,**
**that we do to our Lord.**

—Willard E. Roth, Elkhart, Ind. (adapted). Based on John 3:16; 1 John 4:19; Matt.
6:33; 12:50; 25:40

# 113 Call to Worship

L: Allelulia! Praise, you servants of Yahweh,
  praise the name of Yahweh!

**P: May Yahweh's name be blessed, both now and forever!**

L: From east to west, from north to south,
  praised be the name of Yahweh!

**P: Praise Yahweh, who is good.**
  **Sing praise to God, who is loving.**

L: Yahweh's name stands forever,
  remembered from age to age.

**P: We will sing praises to our God;**
  **we will praise God's name forever.**

L: Great is Yahweh, greatness that is beyond our understanding.

**P: May our mouths speak Yahweh's praise,**
  **and may all creatures bless Yahweh's holy name**
  **forever and ever.**

—Willard E. Roth, Elkhart, Ind. Based on selected psalms (*Yahweh* means *Lord*)

# 114 Antiphonal Praise

L: Praise, O servants of the Lord,
  praise the name of the Lord.

**P: Blessed be the name of the Lord**
  **from this time on and forevermore.**

L: From the rising of the sun to its setting,
  the name of the Lord is to be praised.

**P: The Lord is high above all nations,**
  **and his glory above the heavens.**

L: O sing to the Lord a new song;
  sing to the Lord, all the earth.

**P: Sing to the Lord, bless his name;**
  **tell of his salvation from day to day.**

L: Declare his glory among the nations,
  his marvelous works among all the peoples.

P: **For great is the Lord,**
   **and greatly to be praised;**
   **he is to be revered above all gods.**
*All: Magnify the Lord with me,*
      *and let us exalt his name together.*
      *Blessed be his glorious name forever;*
         *may his glory fill the whole earth.*
      *Amen and Amen.*

—Arlene M. Mark. Based on Pss. 113:1-4; 96:1-4; 34:3; 72:19

# Opening Prayers, Invocations

## 115 Opening Prayer

Creator God,
   we marvel at the world you've given to us.
We're astounded with the depths and breadths of the oceans,
   with the contrasts of acorns and oaks,
   with massive mountains and tiny buds,
   with the vastness of sky and the delicacy of snowflakes,
   with flashing crimson and gold
      amid gentle greens and blues.
We marvel at the earth's resources,
   which sustain all life
   and nourish all growing things.
O Creator God,
   we are grateful and humbled
   that you have made us responsible for this rich earth.
Grant us grace to respect your creation,
   wisdom to conserve its resources,
   and sensitivity to share its wealth.

We enter into our worship today,
> reminded of your generosity and goodness,
> and of our charge to be good stewards,
> in Christ's name. Amen.

—Keith Graber Miller, Goshen, Ind. (adapted)

# 116 Opening Prayer

Creator God,
> you whispered the world into being;
> you sculpted humanity from dust;
> you inspired writers to record the beauty in nature;
> you spoke through artful psalms;
> you placed in us creative spirits.

You are the one, Creating God, whom we worship and serve.
> In your mystery and might, move our creative spirits. Amen.

—Keith Graber Miller, Goshen, Ind. (adapted)

# 117 Invocation

O God,
> we joyously come together to worship,
> realizing we need not summon you into our midst,
> for you are here.

We need not call you into the secret places of our hearts,
> for you are there.

We need
> our eyes of faith to be opened,
>> that we may see you;
> our ears to be unstopped,
>> that we may hear you;
> our minds to be sensitive,
>> that we may know you;
> our hearts to be tender,

that we may receive you.
Grant each one a blessing, O Lord,
   as each has need,
   in the name of Jesus Christ, our Lord. Amen.

—Harry Yoder, in *Prayers for Everyday*, comp. by Elaine Sommers Rich (Newton, Kan.: Faith & Life, 1990), 56 (adapted)

# 118 Invocation

Glorious God,
   we give you our complete adoration.
   Your marvelous love planned the way of salvation.
Tender God,
   we kneel and ask for pardon.
   Your gracious forgiveness restores our souls.
Triumphant God,
   we proclaim your praise.
   Your victorious power defeats death and gives life eternal.
Thanks be to God.

—Arlene M. Mark, MPH Bulletin, 4-12-92 (adapted)

# 119 Invocation

O Lord our God,
   gentle shepherd of the flock,
   in you we find security,
   in you we discover identity.
Before we knew we were lost,
   you searched for us
   and brought us safely to the fold.
We hear your voice, and we come to you.

*(Sing or read verses of the hymn "Ah, Holy Jesus.")*
Lo, the good shepherd for the sheep is offered,
   the slave hath sinned, and the son hath suffered,

for our atonement, while we nothing heedeth,
>God intercedeth.

Therefore, kind Jesus, since we cannot pay thee,
>we do adore thee, and will ever pray thee.
Think on thy pity and thy love unswerving,
>not our deserving. Amen.

—Philip K. Clemens, Goshen, Ind. (adapted). Hymn text, Johann Heermann, trans. by Robert Bridges, *Yattendon Hymnal* (1899; adapted). Based on Pss. 95:6-7; 23; John 10

# 120 Opening Prayer

God, our rock, our refuge, our resting place,
>we come to you.
Out of another busy week of work,
out of our struggles to be meaningful in our world,
out of our desire to meet you and know you
>as the center of our being,
we come to you, O unmovable Rock of our security. Amen.

—Margaret Richer Smith, Lombard, Ill. (adapted)

# 121 Opening Prayer

Great God,
>give us open hearts and minds.
Grant us a vision of you as you are
>and of the world as it might be.
Touch our lips;
>give us words of truth for one another.
Then set us free to do what you ask of us.
>For Jesus' sake. Amen.

—John D. Rempel, New York City

## 122 Opening Prayer

Sovereign God,
we confess that you are Creator of the world;
we confess that Jesus Christ is our only hope in life and death;
we confess that your Spirit bears witness with ours
    that we are your children.
We gather to thank you for the tasks we have to do
    and the resources we give one another.
Draw us together.
    Give us grace to speak the truth freely with each other,
Open our lips so our mouths might show forth your praise.
    In Jesus' name. Amen.

—John D. Rempel, New York City (adapted)

## 123 Opening Prayer

God of grace,
    you have given us minds to know you,
    hearts to love you,
    and voices to sing your praise.
Fill us with your Spirit,
    that we may celebrate your glory
    and truly worship you,
    through Jesus Christ our Lord. Amen.

—John D. Rempel, New York City

## 124 Invocation

Almighty and everlasting God,
    in whom we live and move and have our being,
You have created us for yourself,
    so that our hearts are restless until they rest in you.

Grant unto us purity of heart and strength of purpose,
    so that no selfish passion may hinder us
    from knowing your will,
    and no weakness prevent our doing it.
In your light may we see life clearly,
    and in your service may we find purpose,
    for your mercy's sake. Amen.

—*Minister's Service Book*, ed. by J. D. Morrison (adapted; copyright 1937 by Willett, Clark and Co.; copyright renewed © 1965 by James D. Morrison, Jr.; reprinted by permission of HarperCollins Publishers, Inc.; may not be reproduced or reprinted without permission of HarperCollins)

## 125 Invocation for Evensong

Father of light, Sun of the soul,
when the shadows of twilight fall
    and darkness ends the day,
our thoughts turn to you
    who dwells where night never comes.
We would give to you our evensong
    for the beauty of this day,
    for the Sabbath rest of our spirits,
    for sacred memories and thoughts of your holiness,
    and for this evening hour made serene by your peace.
As stars are seen when the sun goes down,
    and voices are heard in the stillness,
so let us be silent now until your presence grows real,
    and we find our deep desire
    to be a herald of your nearness. Amen.

—*Minister's Service Book*, ed. by J. D. Morrison (copyright 1937 by Willett, Clark and Co.; copyright renewed © 1965 by James D. Morrison, Jr.; reprinted by permission of HarperCollins Publishers, Inc.; may not be reproduced or reprinted without permission of HarperCollins)

## 126 Prayer of Preparation

L: God of all creation,
    we enter your presence,
    humbly aware that all we have and are we owe to you.

**P: We come, desiring to worship together.**
    **Be our inspiration.**

L: We come, desiring to learn together.
    Be our teacher.

**P: We come as eager children, desiring your touch.**
    **Be our loving parent.**

L: Open our eyes,
    that we may see as you see.

**P: Open our hearts,**
    **that we may love as you love.**

L: Open our hands,
    that we may serve as you serve.

*All: In the name of Christ,*
    *our Lord and our example. Amen.*

—Urbane Peachey, Akron (Pa.) Mennonite Church Bulletin, 4-16-92

## 127 Invocation
*(correlate with no. 102)*

L: O Lord our God,
    in this act of worship,
    we glory in your light and love
    made known to us in Jesus Christ.

**P: Come, O light divine, and dispel our human darkness!**

L: Come, O love divine, and melt our hard and loveless hearts!

P: **Make us mirrors of light and models of love;**
**make us partners in your creative acts for all people.**
**Reconcile us to ourselves, to others, and to yourself,**
**as we glory in your light and life. Amen.**

—W. B. J. Martin, *Acts of Worship* (Nashville: Abingdon, 1960), 18 (adapted)

# 128 Invocation

O God of majesty and mystery,
    you are beyond our understanding.
We honor you as Creator God:
    by your word all things visible and invisible came to be.
We honor you as Savior God:
    by your Son all humanity may receive eternal life.
We honor you as Sustainer God:
    by your Spirit we are empowered to live as Christ lived.
Hear our praise, our prayers, our promise
    to honor you joyfully
    in our worship together. Amen.

—Arlene M. Mark

# 129 Invocation

Thanks be to you, O God,
    for this hour of worship and wonder,
    for this day to rest and renew,
    for this time of peace and pardon.
Accept our glory and praise,
    for you are the source of our salvation,
    you are the instructor of righteousness,
    you are our God, and we are your people,
    through Jesus Christ your Son. Amen.

—Arlene M. Mark

# 130 Invocation

Open our eyes, O God, to your worldwide vision.
May we see you at work around the globe
    through the people of God
    committed to reducing injustice.
As your royal priesthood and kingdom followers,
    may we be inspired to join in your reign,
    the reign begun by Jesus, extended by our forebears,
    and continued through us. Amen.

—Keith Graber Miller, Goshen, Ind. Based on 1 Pet. 2:9

# 131 Historic Prayer

O God,  be present with us always;
    dwell within our hearts.
With your light and your Spirit, guide our souls,
    our thoughts, and all our actions,
    that we may teach your Word,
    that your healing power may be in us
    and in your church universal. Amen.

—Melanchthon (1550). Reprinted from *Prayers of the Reformers*, ed. by Clyde
Manschreck (copyright Muhlenberg Press; used by permission of Augsburg
Fortress; may not be reproduced without permission of Augsburg Fortress), 1

# 132 Opening Prayers

*(One or more verses may be used.)*

1.   O God, our Father, we offer you our praise.
    **We celebrate your gracious blessings,**
      **showered upon us anew.**
    You have led us together to teach us your word.
    **Speak to us today,**
    **and give us your grace.**

2. Lord, touch our lips and grant us wisdom,
that we may speak your words of truth.
   **Let our lives be a witness**
   **that will bring honor to you.**
Feed and nourish our hungry souls;
   **yes, give us your food today.**

3. Grant us, Lord, understanding hearts.
May your light of truth burst upon the earth,
   **so all will know your holy Word**
   **and live righteous and godly lives.**
Let the radiant light of your truth
   drive out all darkness and deceit.
**Lead us then, in your everlasting way.**

4. O Lord, the kingdom is yours alone,
   **and the power is also yours.**
Hear this people's praise.
   **We laud your name so holy;**
Bless us with your presence
   throughout this hour of worship.
   **Through Jesus Christ. Amen.**

—Leenaerdt Clock (17th cent.), "Loblied" (Praise hymn), from the *Ausbund*, 131;
trans. by J. C. Wenger, in Paul M. Yoder et al., *Four Hundred Years with the
Ausbund* (HP, 1964), 42. Recommended and adapted by John E. Sharp

# 133  Invocation
*(correlate with no. 98)*

Great God,
   we seek your face as we gather for worship.
Surround us with the power of your presence
   and fill us with the joy of understanding.

Though our lives are a mist that appears for a little while
    and then vanishes,
we thank you for the gift of each moment.
Help us to know the good that is ours to do.
From the mist of our lives, may we gladly give
      many cups of cold water in your name. Amen.

—Ferne Burkhardt, Petersburg, Ont., in MPH Bulletin, 9-29-91 (adapted). Based
  on James 4:14, 17; Matt. 10:42

# 134 Invocation
*(correlate with no. 111)*

Our God, we worship you.
    We praise and we adore you.
    We offer you thanksgiving.
Together, assembled as we are in this time and place,
    we hear you in word,
    and we hear you in silence.
    We listen, we sing, we pray.
Thank you for the opportunity
    of this time of worship,
    and these moments of silence before you.
*(brief silence)*
    Amen.

—Roy Umble, Goshen, Ind.

# 135 Invocation

Our Lord and God,
    Maker of heaven and earth,
    tender shepherd of the flock,
our praise is due to you
    for your work in our lives;
      sometimes healing,

> sometimes comforting,
> sometimes convicting,
> sometimes pushing
> beyond the familiar and secure.

Do your work among us today. Amen.

—John E. Sharp, Middlebury, Ind.

# 136 Opening Prayer

O holy God,
> high above us yet present within us,
> assist us in drawing near to you.

Let us sense the awesomeness of One beyond us,
> the fear of your righteousness,
> the depth of our darkness in your light.

In your presence may we feel your tender love,
> hear your vow of guidance,
> be changed by your truth,
> and receive your blessing.

Accept our meager attempts at worship,
> that we may be worthy of your presence. Amen.

—J. Wayne Judd, *Prayers for Public Worship*, ed. by Edward K. Ziegler (Elgin, Ill.: Brethren Press, 1986), 12

# 137 Invocation

O God,
we your people have gathered
> to worship you and celebrate
> our liberation from sin and death.

We acknowledge you as the source of our being,
> though we do not comprehend
> the depths of your mercy and love for us.

We pray that your Spirit will lead us in worship
    as you have led your people
    throughout all time. Amen.

—Rebecca Slough, in *Prayers for Public Worship*, Edward K. Ziegler (Elgin, Ill.:
Brethren, 1986), 14 (adapted)

## 138 Prayer

O holy God, you have taught us
    that if we do not love our neighbor, whom we have seen,
    we cannot love God, whom we have not seen.
Forbid that we would come to you with dishonest worship.
May what we pray be what we practice:
    We ask for your forgiveness;
      help us to be forgiving.
    We seek your mercy;
      help us to be merciful.
    We say we love you;
      let us see in others all that may be loveable.
For we cannot find you in worship
    unless we find you in those
    for whom your Son lived and died. Amen.

—Adapted from *Lift Up Your Hearts* by Walter Russell Bowie (copyright renewal
© 1984 by Mrs. Jean B. Evans, Mrs. Elizabeth Chapman, and Mrs. Walter
Russell Bowie, Jr.; used by permission of Abingdon Press)

## Affirming the Faith

## 139 Affirmation of Faith

True evangelical faith cannot lie dormant,
    but expresses itself
    in all righteousness and works of love.

It dies unto the flesh and blood;
    it destroys all forbidden lusts and desires;
    it clothes the naked; it feeds the hungry;
    it comforts the sorrowful;
    it shelters the destitute;
    it aids and consoles the sad;
    it returns good for evil;
    it serves those that harm it;
    it prays for those that persecute it;
    it teaches, admonishes, and reproves,
      with the Word of the Lord;
    it seeks that which is lost;
    it binds up that which is wounded;
    it heals that which is diseased,
    and it saves that which is sound.

It has become all things to all people.

—Menno Simons (ca. 1539), MPH Bulletin, 1-25-87. Based on *Complete Writings of M.S.*, ed. by J. C. Wenger, trans. by L. Verduin (HP, 1956), 307

## 140 Affirmation of Faith from the Writings of John

We believe that God is Spirit,
    and they that worship Him
    must worship Him in spirit and in truth.
  That God is Light,
    and that if we walk in the light, as He is in the light,
    we have fellowship one with another.
  That God is Love,
    and that everyone that loves is born of God
    and knows God.
We believe that Jesus Christ is the Son of God,
    and that God has given to us eternal life,
    and this life is in His Son.

That He is the Resurrection and the Life,
   and that whoever believes on Him,
   though he were dead, yet shall he live.
We believe that the Holy Spirit has come
   and convinces the world of sin,
   righteousness, and judgment;
   that He guides us into all truth.
We believe that we are children of God,
   and that He has given us of His Spirit.
We believe that if we confess our sins,
      He is faithful and just to forgive us our sins,
      and to cleanse us from all unrighteousness.
We believe that the world passes away and the lust thereof,
      but he that does the will of God abides forever.

—From *Book of Common Worship* by Wilbur P. Thirkield (copyright 1932 by
   Gilbert Thirkield; copyright © renewed 1960; used by permission of Dutton
   Signet, a division of Penguin Books USA Inc)

# 141  Statement of Belief and Purpose

We believe that Jesus Christ
   is the expression of God's love for all people.
Therefore, we pledge our loyalty to him
   and his way of life.

We accept the New Testament as the guidebook
   to abundant Christian living.
Therefore, we pledge ourselves to study its message
   for our day and follow the light we discover.

We believe that communion with God and fellowship with
   Christ are essential to daily living and spiritual growth.
Therefore, we will devote time regularly
   to personal devotions, family worship, and meditation.

We believe that God is our Creator
   and all men and women are our brothers and sisters.

Therefore, as we attempt to live Christ's way of reconciling love,
    we can consider no one our enemy,
    we dare not hate, we cannot kill.

We believe that spiritual values
    are more important than material possessions.
Therefore, we will live modestly, dress simply,
    and eat temperately, in order to place God's kingdom first.

—From the Church of the Brethren National Youth Cabinet (1948), adapted in *For All Who Minister* (copyright © 1993, Brethren Press, Elgin, Ill.; used by permission)

# 142 Litany of Affirmation

L: I, Paul, handed on to you as of first importance
        what I in turn had received:
        that Christ died for our sins
        in accordance with the Scriptures.

**P: By God's grace, I am what I am.**

L: Christ was buried and on the third day was raised,
        in accordance with the Scriptures.

**P: By God's grace, I am what I am.**

L: Christ appeared to Cephas, then to the twelve,
        then to more than five hundred at one time,
        then to James and all the apostles.

**P: By God's grace, I am what I am.**

L: God's grace was not in vain;
        so we preach and so we believe.

**P: By God's grace, I am what I am.**

—James G. Kirk, *When We Gather: Year C* (Philadelphia: Geneva, 1985; used by permission of Westminister John Knox Press), 40-41. Based on 1 Cor. 15:3-11

# 143 Affirmation of Faith for the Church

We believe that God has established the church,
    and will preserve and protect it
    as a corporate reflection of God's presence among us,
    providing a foretaste of our glorious hope.
We believe that Jesus Christ is the head of the church
    and died to come alive in true resurrection,
    even as we die to sin and live to life eternal
    in baptism into Christ's body.
We believe that the Holy Spirit breathed fire and life
    into the church at Pentecost
    and still provides redeeming power
    for its preservation and ministry.
We believe in the fellowship of all saints
    who have responded in faith to Jesus Christ
    and who affirm loyalty to God above all else
    in life and death.
We believe each member is called
    to live faithfully as Jesus lived
    by loving and serving others,
    demonstrating the new creation in Christ.
We believe the church is a community of disciples,
    using gifts freely and wisely
    for the common good of the body
    and to advance the gospel of Jesus Christ
    until he comes again.

—Arlene M. Mark

# 144 Affirming the Faith

L: We celebrate the resurrected Jesus, who lives among us,

P: **whose Spirit empowers us to remove barriers,**
**tear down walls, heal divisions,**
**and seek shalom without and within.**

L: We celebrate the resurrected Jesus, who lives among us,

P: **whose Spirit empowers us**
**to see our sister's good as our own,**
**to be our brother's advocate,**
**to love our neighbor as ourselves,**
**and to contribute to the well-being**
**of every part of Christ's body,**

All: *so that indeed we can build up, and grow up,*
*and be joined together into a new structure:*
*where Christ's Spirit dwells,*
*where Christ's Spirit empowers us*
*to be shalom-seekers, shalom-finders, and shalom-makers!*

—Margaret Richer Smith, Lombard, Ill. (adapted; *shalom* means *peace*)

# 145 A Creed

L: We are not alone, we live in God's world.

P: **We believe in God,**
**who has created and is creating,**
**who has come in Jesus to reconcile**
**and to make all things new.**

**We trust in God,**
**who calls us to be the church;**
**to celebrate God's presence,**
**to live with respect in creation,**
**to love and serve others,**
**to seek justice and to resist evil,**
**to proclaim Jesus, crucified and risen,**
**our judge and our hope.**

**In life, in death, in life beyond death,
God is with us.**

**We are not alone. Thanks be to God.**

—The United Church of Canada

# 146 A Prayer for Keeping Faith

O Keeper of Faith,
    help us to keep the faith entrusted to us:
    faith in a world worth saving,
    faith in a dream worth sharing,
    faith in a heritage worth keeping
    even as we reinvigorate it
    to have meaning for us now.
Help us keep faith in you,
    and help us not lose faith in ourselves,
    for faith is the substance of our hope,
    and hope is the assurance of love.
Praise to you, O Faithful One,
    now and forever. Amen.

—Miriam T. Winter, *WomanWisdom* (New York: Crossroad, 1991), 168 (adapted)

# 147 Confession That Jesus Is Lord

We confess that Jesus is Lord;
    what we believe in our hearts
    we confess with our lips, and so we are saved.

We confess that Jesus is Lord;
    we have died to self, and our lives
    are hid with Christ in God.

We confess that Jesus is Lord;
    we set our minds on things above,
    not on things here on earth.

We confess that Jesus is Lord;
>   we put off our old self
>   and put on the new,
>   created in God's likeness.

We confess that Jesus is Lord;
>   whatever we do, we do in the name
>   of the Lord Jesus Christ, with thanksgiving.

We confess that Jesus is Lord;
>   we belong to God,
>   for God has bought us with a price.

We confess that Jesus is Lord;
>   he will come again and receive us unto himself;
>   that where he is, we may be also.

We confess with our mouths and believe in our hearts
>   that Jesus is Lord, to be glory of God,
>   now and evermore. Amen.

—Arlene M. Mark, in MPH Bulletin, 3-8-92 (adapted). Based on Deut. 26:1-11;
   Ps. 91:9-16; Rom. 10:8b-13; Eph. 4:24; Luke 4:1-13; 1 Cor. 6:19-20

# 148 Confession of Faith

*(unison reading)*

We believe in God the Creator of all,
>   known to us through perfect love,
>   who has called forth a people of faith.

We believe in Jesus Christ, the Word become flesh,
>   crucified and resurrected,
>   our Savior from sin, our peace, and Lord of the church.

We believe in the Holy Spirit,
>   poured out on all believers,
>   our source of inspiration and power.

We respond to Christ in faith as the church,
>   the community sustained by the Spirit,
>   called to proclaim and witness to the kingdom of God.

We continue the mission of Christ,
    making disciples, forgiving and restoring sinners,
    baptizing believers, sharing the Lord's Supper,
    using our gifts in unity and love.

We commit ourselves to follow Jesus Christ,
    growing by grace into the image of God.
We accept God's call to live in the Spirit as faithful disciples,
    practicing purity, stewardship, justice and peace,
    and loving friend and enemy.

We joyfully worship God, the three-in-one,
    giving allegiance to Christ as Lord.
We believe in God's everlasting reign,
    in victory over evil, in the resurrection of the dead,
    in Christ's coming again in judgment and glory.
To God be praise forever and ever. Amen!

—Based on "Confession of Faith in a Mennonite Perspective" (1995)

# Praising the Lord

## 149 Adoration

L: Praise our God, all servants,
    for the Lord our God the Almighty reigns.
**P: Let us rejoice and be glad and give God glory.**
L: Holy, Holy, Holy, Lord God Almighty,
    who was and is and is to come.
**P: You are worthy, our Lord and God,**
    **to receive glory and honor and power,**
    **for you created all things,**
    **and by your will they existed and were created.**
L: Great and amazing are your deeds,
    Lord God the Almighty!
**P: Just and true are your ways, King of the nations!**

L: You alone are holy.
    All nations will come and worship before you,
    for your judgments have been revealed.
**P: Salvation and glory and power to you, our God,**
    **for your judgments are true and just.**
    **Praise to you, Lord God Almighty.**

—Arlene M. Mark. Based on Rev. 4:8, 11; 15:3-4; 19:1-2, 5-7

# 150  Litany of Praise

L: Praise be to you, O Lord,
    who spins shining stars across the wondrous heavens,
    and stretches out the seas;
**P: who lifts the dawn into place**
    **and sets boundaries for night;**
L: who awes the earth with storms
    and gentles it with rainbows;
**P: who gives everything a season**
    **and breathes life and love into the dust of us,**
*All: Praise be to you, O Lord.*

L: Praise be to you, O Lord,
    in all times and for all things:
**P: the soft slant of sunlight, the evening breeze,**
    **the sweat of labor, a sweet song to lighten the heart;**
L: the deep breath, the tended wound,
    mercy, quietness, a friend;
**P: for the miracles of the daily**
    **and the mysteries of the eternal,**
*All: Praise be to you, O Lord.*

L: Praise be to you, O Lord,
    from all creatures:
        laughers and list-makers,
        wonderers and worriers,
        poets and plodders and prophets,

P: **the wrinkled, the newborn,**
   **the whale, and the worm—**
**from all, and from us,**
*All: Praise, praise be to you*
       *for the amazing grace*
       *through Jesus Christ our Lord. Amen.*

—Excerpted from the book *Guerillas of Grace*, by Ted Loder (copyright © 1984 by LuraMedia; reprinted by permission of LuraMedia, Inc., San Diego)

# 151 Adoration, Thanksgiving, and Commitment

O Lord God, we bless you.
   All that is within us blesses your holy name.
We remember all your benefits to us:
   You forgive our iniquities, you heal our diseases,
   you redeem our lives from the depths of depravity,
   you crown us with steadfast love and mercy,
   and satisfy us with good as long as we live.
We thank you for remembering us,
   for responding to our cries from oppression.
We thank you for acting on behalf of all
   who continue to cry for help.
May our ears be your ears; our eyes, your eyes;
   our hands, your hands; and our hearts, your heart.
O God, in your presence we know we are yours;
   we open ourselves to you in this holy silence. Amen.

—Philip K. Clemens, Goshen, Ind. Based on Ps. 103

# 152 Prayer of Praise

L: From before the world began
   and after the end of eternity,
P: **You are God.**

L: From the sea bursting out of the deep
    to the wind ceasing from its chase,

**P: You are God.**

L: In the constancy of created things
    and in their rhythms of change,

**P: You are God.**

L: In the vastness of the universe
    and the forgotten corner of our hearts,

**P: You are God.**

*All:    You are our God, and we bless you.*

L: Because the world is beautiful,
    and beauty is a tender thing,
    and we are stewards of creation,
  We need you, God.

**P: We need you, God.**

L: Because human knowledge seems endless,
    the world is our oyster,
    and we do not know what we do not know,
  We need you, God.

**P: We need you, God.**

L: Because we can live without you,
    and are free to go against you,
    and could worship our wisdom alone,
  We need you, God.

**P: We need you, God.**

L: Because you came among us, and sat beside us,
    and heard us speak and saw us ignore you,
    and healed our pain and let us wound you,
    and loved us to the end,
    and triumphed over all our hatred,
  We need you, God.

**P: We need you, God.**

L: Because you, not we, are God, we need you, God.

P: **We need you, God.** *(silence)*

L: Listen, for the Lord who created you says,
>"Do not be afraid, For I have redeemed you.
>I have called you by name—you are mine.
>You are precious to me.
>I love you. I honor you. I am with you." *(silence)*

L: Listen, Lord, it is your people who say:

P: **We are your children, the creatures of your care,**
>**the bearers of your image.**
>**This day, we will walk by your light,**
>**live by your Spirit, and follow your Son.**
>**This day, we will not offer to you**
>**offerings that cost us nothing.**
>**For this is the day that the Lord has made.**
>**We will rejoice and be glad in it. Amen.**

—John L. Bell, in *A Wee Worship Book* (© 1988 Wild Goose Worship Group, Iona Community, Glasgow G51 3UU, Scotland; adapted). Based on Gen. 1; John 1:10-11; 13:1; Isa. 43:1; 2 Sam. 24:24; Ps. 119:24

# Prayers of Confession

## 153 Prayer of Confession

Most merciful God,
>we confess that we have sinned against you
>in thought, word, and deed,
>by what we have done,
>and by what we have left undone.

We have not loved you with our whole heart;
>we have not loved our neighbors as ourselves.

We are truly sorry and we humbly repent.

For the sake of your Son Jesus Christ,
>have mercy on us and forgive us;

that we may delight in your will,
and walk in your ways,
to the glory of your name. Amen.

—*Book of Common Prayer According to the Use of the Episcopal Church* (New York: The Church Hymnal Corp., 1979), 352

# 154 **Congregational Prayer of Confession**

O faithful God,
keeper of an everlasting covenant,
we confess that we are a faithless people;
again and again we turn away from you.
Left to ourselves,
we would gain the whole world
and lose our souls.
Forgive our sin.
*(time for silent intercession or stating suitable corporate requests)*
Restore us in mercy, O God;
teach us to be faithful and true,
to love you above all else
through Jesus Christ our Lord. Amen.

—Marlene Kropf, Elkhart, Ind. Based on Matt. 16:26; Mark 8:36; Luke 9:25

# 155 **Prayer of Confession**

8-25-2013

L: Let us confess our sin to God and to each other.
P: **Merciful God,**
**We confess that we have often failed**
**to be an obedient church.**
**We have not done your will,**
**we have broken your law,**
**we have rebelled against your love.**

> **We have not loved our neighbors**
> **nor forgiven our enemies.**
> **We have trusted in weapons**
> **rather than trusting in you.**
> **We have neglected the power of the Spirit**
> **given at Pentecost.**
> **Forgive us, we pray, and free us for joyful obedience;**
> **through Jesus Christ our Lord. Amen.**

*(words of assurance)*

L: Once we were alienated from God because of our evil.
But now God has reconciled us by Christ's death
to present us holy, without blemish,
and free from accusation!
Continue in faith, established and firm,
unmoved from the hope held out in the gospel.

P: **Thanks be to God.**

—Dan Schrock, Columbus, Ohio. Based on Col. 1:21-23; Eph 5:27

# 156 Prayer of Confession

L: O God, in your goodness have mercy on us;

P: **in your great tenderness wipe away our faults.**

L: Wash us clean of our guilt,

P: **purify us from our sin.**

L: We are well aware of our faults,
we have our sin constantly in mind.

P: **Purify us until we are clean;**
**wash us until we are whiter than snow.**

L: O God, create clean hearts in us
and put into us new and constant spirits.

P: **Do not banish us from your presence;**
**do not deprive us of your holy spirit.**

L: Be our savior again, renew our joy.

P: **Keep our spirits steady and willing,**
   **and our lives shall teach transgressors the way to you.**
*All: Save us from death, God our Savior,*
   *and our mouths will speak out your praise.*

—Arlene M. Mark. Based on Ps. 51, JB

# 157 Prayer of Confession

Almighty and everlasting God, we know that your love
   is over every creature whom your hands have made.
We know that your only wish is not to destroy but to save,
   not to condemn but to forgive.
And we know that, to receive your forgiveness,
   we need only bring a penitent and contrite heart.
Save us from all that would hinder us
   from having a godly sorrow for our sins;
   from blindness, which is not aware that we are sinning;
   from pride, which cannot admit that we are wrong;
   from self-will, which can see nothing but our own way;
   from self-righteousness, which can see no flaw within us;
   from callousness, which has sinned so often
      that we cease to care;
   from defiance, which is not even sorry for our sins;
   from evasion, which puts the blame
      on someone or something else;
   from hearts so hardened that we cannot repent.

Make us responsive always:
   with eyes which are open to our own faults;
   with a conscience which is sensitive and quick to warn;
   with a heart which cannot sin in peace;
   with a spirit which is moved to regret and remorse.

Grant that with true repentance we may be truly forgiven,
so that as we experience your graciousness and compassion,
we find your love great enough to cover all our sin;
through Jesus Christ our Lord. Amen.

—William Barclay, *Prayers for the Christian Year* (London: SCM Press, 1964), 46-47 (adapted). Based on Joel 2:12-17

# 158 Prayer of Confession

*All: All we like sheep have gone astray;*
*we have turned to our own way.*

L: We have wandered in restlessness and busyness,
far from your pastures and waters.
Our souls are troubled.

P: **Gather us, Lord.**

L: We have preferred our own paths
and put our own names first.

P: **Lead us, Lord.**

L: We fear evil and death around us and within us.

P: **Comfort us, Lord.**

L: We are hungry and empty, wounded and thirsty.

P: **Feed us, anoint us, Lord.**

L: All we like sheep have gone astray;
we have turned to our own way.
And the Lord has laid on Christ the sins of us all.

P: **Forgive us, Lord.** *(silence)*

L: Surely God's goodness and mercy follow us
all the days of our lives,
and we are invited into the house of God's presence,
this day, and forever.

*All: The Lord is our shepherd.*
*We shall not want!*

—Nina B. Lanctot, Elkhart, Ind., in Fellowship of Hope Bulletin, 9-4-93 (adapted). Based on Isa. 53:6; Ps. 23

# 159 Prayer of Repentance

Lord Jesus Christ,
 you are the way of peace.
Come into the brokenness of our lives and our land
 with your healing love.
Help us to bow before you in true repentance,
 and to bow to one another in true repentance.

By the fire of your Holy Spirit,
 melt our hard hearts
 and consume the pride and prejudice which separate us.
Fill us, O Lord, with your perfect love,
 which casts out our fear,
 and bind us together in that unity
 which you share with the Father
 and the Holy Spirit forever. Amen.

—Cecil Kerr, Christian Renewal Centre, Rostrevor, Northern Ireland (adapted)

# 160 Prayer for Wholeness

Righteous God,
your mercy awaits us when we return to you
 in meekness and repentance.
Cleanse us from selfishness and falseness,
 which separate us from your fellowship.
Through your atoning love,
 heal the brokenness in our lives and in our world.
With wholeness restored,
 help us live for the coming of your Son, our Savior,
 in whose name we pray. Amen.

—Arlene M. Mark, in MPH Bulletin, 12-5-82 (adapted)

## 161 Prayer of Confession

Holy God, you have called us to be holy,
    even as you are holy.
We confess that we have not lived
    the disciples' life to which you have called us.
We have ignored our pledge to take up the cross
    and follow in joyful obedience.
We have become more conformed to the world
    than transformed by new minds and natures.
We have relaxed our principles
    and justified personal pleasure.
Forgive our unholiness, our unfaithfulness to you.
Empower us to be worthy disciples
    who follow the teachings of Jesus and grow in his image.
Help us live as a called-out people,
    holy and acceptable in your sight,
    to whom be glory forever and ever. Amen.

—Arlene M. Mark

## 162 Prayer of Confession

Almighty God,
we confess that we are often swept up
    in the tide of our generation.
We have failed to be your holy people,
    set apart for your divine purpose.
We live more in apathy of fatalism than in passion of hope.
We are moved more by private ambition
    than by concern for social justice.
We dream more of privilege and benefits
    than of service and sacrifice.
We speak in your name without nourishing our souls,
    without relying on your grace.

Help us to make room in our hearts and lives for you.
Forgive us, revive us, reshape us in your image. Amen.

—Lydia S. Martinez, from *United Methodist Clergywoman's Consultation Resource Book* (1987), 57 (adapted)

# 163  Prayer of Confession

*(in unison)*
Lord, we bow before you,
    aware of our unworthiness to be called
    your sons and daughters.
We confess
    that we are tempted by power, wealth,
      and illusions of security,
      which lead us away from you;
    that we have passively and actively
      participated in exploiting others
      created in your image;
    that we have hidden behind our inhibitions and fears
      to avoid living disciplined lives;
    that we have depended on our wisdom to govern the world
      and failed to acknowledge your kingship;
    that we have played the role of judge
      when only you could judge;
    that we have neglected the causes of peace,
      love, and justice in our lives.
We ask that you attend to each of us
    as we silently make our confessions.
*(silence)*
Lord, we rejoice that you have not abandoned us,
    though we are unworthy.
You sent your Son to redeem us
    and through his death and resurrection
    brought our redemption.

With thanksgiving we proclaim your love and grace
>    shown to us in Jesus
>    and together confess him as our Redeemer.
In his name we pray. Amen.

—Rebecca Slough, *Prayers for Public Worship*, ed by Edward K Ziegler (Elgin Ill ·
Brethren Press, 1986), 17 (adapted)

# 164 A Litany of Confession and Assurance

L: Let us make confession to God the Lord,
>    each of us acknowledging our sins and wrongdoings.
>    Let us pray:
**P: Almighty God,**
>    **we confess that we are inclined to do evil**
>    **and slow to do good,**
>    **and that we more and more separate ourselves from you.**
>    **We have not believed your Word**
>    **nor followed your holy commandments.**
>    **Be gracious unto us, we beseech you,**
>    **and forgive our iniquity.**
*(silence while each person presents petitions and requests to God)*
L: Hear the words of assurance given to all
>    who turn in faith to Christ our Savior:
>    God so loved the world that he gave his only Son,
>    so that everyone who believes in him may not perish
>    but may have eternal life.
>    The saying is sure and worthy of full acceptance,
>    that Christ Jesus came into the world to save sinners.

—Martin Bucer (1524), from "The Strasbourg Liturgy," in *Book of Worship* (Elgin,
Ill.: Brethren Press, 1964), 79 (adapted; litany copyright holder unknown).
Based on Rom. 3:9-20; John 3:16; 1 Tim. 1:15

# 165 Litany of Reconciliation

*All have sinned and fallen short of the glory of God.*

L: The hatred which divides nation from nation,
    race from race, class from class:

**P: Father forgive.**

L: The covetous desires of people and nations
    to possess what is not their own:

**P: Father forgive.**

L: The greed which exploits the work of human hands
    and lays waste the earth:

**P: Father forgive.**

L: Our envy of the welfare and happiness of others:

**P: Father forgive.**

L: Our indifference to the plight
    of the imprisoned, the homeless and the refugee:

**P: Father forgive.**

L: The lust which dishonours
    the bodies of men, women and children:

**P: Father forgive.**

L: The pride which leads us to trust in ourselves
    and not in God:

**P: Father forgive.**

*All: Be kind to one another, tenderhearted,*
    *forgiving one another, as God in Christ forgave you.*

—Coventry Cathedral Pamphlets (© the Provost and Chapter of Coventry
Cathedral). Based on Rom. 3:23; Eph. 4:32

# 166 Litany of Confession for the Family

L: O God, the Father of us all,
   we come to you in sorrow, for we have failed you.

*All: Lord, forgive us, and help us to obey.*

L: You have taught us all:
   Honor your father and mother, that it may go well with you
   and that you may enjoy long life on the earth.

*All: We have sometimes failed you.*
   *Lord, forgive us, and help us to obey.*

L: You have taught us as children:
   Obey your parents in the Lord, for this is right.

*All:   We have sometimes failed you.*
   *Lord, forgive us, and help us to obey.*

L: You have taught us as fathers:
   Do not exasperate your children;
   instead, bring them up in the training
   and instruction of the Lord.

**Fathers: We have sometimes failed you.**
   **Lord, forgive us, and help us to obey.**

L: You have taught us as mothers to live with sincere faith
   and bring our children to Christ.

**Mothers: We have sometimes failed you.**
   **Lord, forgive us, and help us to obey.**

L: You have taught us as husbands:
   Love your wives as you love yourselves.

**Husbands: We have sometimes failed you.**
   **Lord, forgive us, and help us to obey.**

L: You have taught us as wives:
   Respect your husbands.

**Wives: We have sometimes failed you.**
   **Lord, forgive us, and help us to obey.**

L: You have taught us as the Christian family:
   Submit to one another
   out of reverence for Christ.

*All: We have sometimes failed you.*

*Lord, forgive us, and help us to obey.*

*Father, turn our hearts to one another*
*so that others will be attracted by our joy*
*and many will be added to your church. Amen.*

## Assurance of Forgiveness

# 167 Words of Assurance

*(After confession, one of these Scriptures may be introduced and read.)*

L: Hear the comforting words given to us in the Scriptures.
   *(or)* Be assured that God hears our prayers and forgives us.

1. If we walk in the light, as God is in the light,
   we have fellowship with one another,
   and the blood of Jesus the Son
   cleanses us from all sin. *(based on 1 John 1:7)*

2. If we confess our sins,
   God who is faithful and just
   will forgive us our sins and cleanse us
   from all unrighteousness. *(based on 1 John 1:9)*

3. If anyone sins, we have someone
   who pleads with the Father on our behalf—
   Jesus Christ, the righteous one.
   Christ himself is the means
   by which our sins are forgiven,
   and not our sins only,
   but the sins of the whole world. *(based on 1 John 2:1-2, TEV)*

4. God so loved the world that he gave his only Son,
   so that everyone who believes in him

may not perish but have eternal life. *(based on John 3:16)*

5. Christ himself bore our sins in his body on the cross,
   so that, free from sins, we might live in righteousness;
   by his wounds we have been healed. *(based on 1 Peter 2:24)*

6. This saying is sure and worthy of full acceptance,
   that Christ Jesus came into the world
   to save sinners. *(based on 1 Tim. 1:15)*

7. There is therefore now no condemnation
   for those who are in Christ Jesus,
   who walk not according to the flesh
   but according to the Spirit. *(based on Rom. 8:1, 4)*

8. Jesus our Lord was handed over to death for our trespasses
   and raised for our justification. *(based on Rom. 4:25)*

9. Therefore, since we are justified by faith,
   we have peace with God through our Lord Jesus Christ,
   through whom we have obtained access to this grace
   in which we stand. *(based on Rom. 5:1)*

10. The sacrifice acceptable to God is a broken spirit;
    a broken spirit and contrite heart, O God,
    you will not despise. *(based on Ps. 51:17)*

11. The Lord is gracious and merciful, slow to anger
    and abounding in steadfast love. *(based on Ps. 145:8)*

12. When the righteous cry for help, the Lord hears,
    and rescues them from all their troubles.
    The Lord is near to the brokenhearted,
    and saves the crushed in spirit. *(based on Ps. 34:17-18)*

13. Evil brings death to the wicked,
    and those who hate the righteous will be condemned.
    The Lord redeems the life of his servants;
    none of those who take refuge in him
    will be condemned. *(based on Ps. 34:21-22)*

14. Blessed be the Lord,
    who daily bears us up;
    God is our salvation.
    Our God is a God of salvation, and to God, the Lord,
    belongs escape from death. *(based on Ps. 68:19-20)*

15. Seek the Lord while he may be found,
    call upon him while he is near;
    let the wicked forsake their way,
    and the unrighteous their thoughts;
    let them return to the Lord,
    that he may have mercy on them, and to our God,
    for he will abundantly pardon. *(based on Isa. 55:6-7)*

16. Come now, let us argue it out, says the Lord;
    though your sins are like scarlet,
    they shall be like snow;
    though they are red like crimson,
    they shall become like wool. *(based on Isa. 1:18)*

17. All we like sheep have gone astray;
    we have turned to our own way, and the Lord
    has laid on him the iniquity of us all. *(based on Isa. 53:6)*

18. Because Jesus lives forever, he has a permanent priesthood.
    Therefore, he is able to save completely
    those who come to God through him,
    to save those who approach God through him,
    because he always lives to intercede for them.
                         *(based on Heb. 7:24-25, NIV)*

## 168 A Future Where Forgiveness Is Waiting

We give thanks to you, God our Father,
    for mercy that reaches out,
    for patience that waits our returning,
    and for your love that is ever ready
    to welcome sinners.
**We praise you that in Christ Jesus**
    **you meet us with grace, embrace us in acceptance,**
    **and affirm us as citizens of a forgiven universe.**
We give thanks to you that by your Holy Spirit
    you move us to change direction, receive your love,
    and become what we most truly are.
**In darkness and in light, in trouble and in joy,**
    **help us then, O God, to accept your forgiveness,**
    **to believe your love, and to trust your purpose.**
Through Christ Jesus our Lord. **Amen.**

—Terry Falla, in *Be Our Freedom, Lord*, ed. by Terry Falla, 2d ed. (Adelaide: Open Book Publishers, 1994), 136. Based on Luke 15:11-32

## Pre-Sermon Prayers

## 169 Prayer for Illumination

Christ our teacher,
    you reach into our lives
    not through instruction, but story.
Open our hearts to be attentive;
    that seeing, we may perceive,
    that hearing, we may understand,
    that understanding, we may act;
    in your name. Amen.

—Janet Morley, *All Desires Known* (Wilton, Conn.: Morehouse-Barlow, 1989), 12 (adapted)

# 170 Prayer of Preparation

Ruler of earth and heaven,
    let your servants deliver your words with all boldness.
Stretch out your hand to heal.
Perform signs and wonders
    through the name of your holy servant Jesus.
Fill us with his Spirit that we may be changed. Amen.

—John D. Rempel, New York City (adapted). Based on Acts 4:24-31

# 171 Prayer Before Scripture or Sermon

Gracious God,
we have come in search of Christ,
    the author of life.
Open the Scriptures to us
    that we might see him as he is
    and meet him face to face. Amen.

—John D. Rempel, New York City

# 172 Petition for Wisdom

*(in unison)*

O God, grant us heavenly wisdom in all that we think and do;
    for your wisdom is first pure, then peaceable,
    gentle, willing to yield,
    full of mercy and good fruits,
    without a trace of partiality or hypocrisy.
We give thanks, O God,
    for the harvest of peace and justice
    that is sown in wisdom by those who love you
    amid disorder and wickedness of every kind.
We pray that we may be wise and understanding
    in our life circumstances,
    through the grace of Jesus Christ our Lord. Amen.

—Urbane Peachey, Akron, Pa. (adapted). Based on James 3:17-18

# 173 Prayer of Illumination

O God,
By your spoken Word,
> you created everything that is.
By your incarnate Word,
> you redeemed us.
By your comforting Word,
> you are with us still.
Prepare us now
> to hear your Word to us this day.

—*Peacemaking Through Worship*, vol. 2, ed. by Jane Parker Huber (Louisville: Presbyterian Church, USA, Mar. 1993), 107 (adapted)

# Prayers of Thanksgiving

## 174 Thanksgiving for Our Congregation

L: We give thanks for remembered times
> when we have shared in worship, in learning, in service,
> and in fun with members of our faith community.

**P: We give thanks to God.**

L: We remember friendships made, celebrations enjoyed,
> moments of nurture, and kindnesses done.

**P: We give thanks to God.**

L: We rejoice for expectations met, gifts given,
> promises kept, support received.

**P: We give thanks to God.**

L: We also remember gifts not given, wounds not healed,
> failures not confessed, vows not honored.

**P: We confess our sin.**

L: We recognize all those who have enriched our congregation
> and are now gone from among us to be with God
> or to serve Christ in other places.
> For all their blessings,

P: **We give thanks to God.**

L: We offer our wisdom and experience,
    our competence and compassion,
    our love, and our abilities in service and thanksgiving.

P: **We give ourselves in thanks to God.**

—Alice M. Price, La Jara, Colo., Litany for La Jara Voluntary-Service Reunion;
  from Pilgrims Mennonite Church, Akron, Pa. (adapted)

# 175 Thanksgiving for Creation

L: Alive! We thank you, Lord,
    whose finger touched our dust
    and gave us breath.

P: **We thank you, Lord,**
  **who gave us sight and sense**
    **to see the flowers,**
    **to hear the wind,**
    **to feel the waters in our hand,**

L:    to sleep with the night
    and wake with the sun,
    to stand upon this earth,
    to hear your voice,
    to sing your praise.

P: **Our hearts are stirred**
    **with each new sight and sound.**

L: Like a stream the whole world pours
    into our lives, and eyes, and hands,

P: **and fills our souls**
    **with the joy of gratitude**
    **and living gladness.**

L: We want to embrace
    and experience and express
    every good thing in your world.

P:  **O Lord, our God,
how excellent is your name.**

—Terry Falla, in *Be Our Freedom, Lord,* ed. by Terry Falla (Adelaide: Lutheran
Publishing House, 1984), 68

# 176  Prayer of Thanksgiving

Lord God, you are the King of the universe.
Your goodness does not change
from one generation to the next.
You let rain fall on the just and the unjust.
We praise you that you never give up
loving us and our world.

Today we thank you:
that we may gather to worship
without fear or intimidation;
that fruit and grain have ripened
to give us food for another year;
that people have entered our lives
and taught us to love, hope, and dream;
that we have strong minds and bodies
to make our world more human;
that we have a social order
where fairness and dissent have a place;
that salvation is ours now and eternally.

We pray for those who suffer
when creation breaks down,
when people have no harvest,
when there is no love.
Be merciful, O God,
to those who need mercy.
Push us to be merciful,
for you have been merciful.

Accept our thanks,
>we pray for Jesus' sake. Amen.

—John D. Rempel, in *Prayers for Everyday*, comp. by Elaine Sommers Rich
(Newton, Kan., 1990), 70 (adapted)

# 177 Thanksgiving Prayer

Almighty God,
>source of all life, giver of all that is good,
>we gather to offer our praise and thanks.

The richness of our lives,
>when we stop to take measure,
>is more than we can comprehend.

We have blessings of joy and hope,
>the challenge to labor and the luxury of leisure.

Your world is full of wonder, and its beauty delights us.

We praise your generosity
>and confess that we are ungenerous receivers.

We are slow to share and quick to squander.

We take for granted what we have and anticipate more.

Give us an awareness of our blessings
>so that we will share joyously and live responsibly.

Give us a sense of self-worth
>so that getting things does not usurp other values.

For all your goodness, let us express our gratitude
>by genuinely caring for our world
>through the grace of Jesus Christ. Amen.

—Arlene M. Mark

## 178 Prayer

Dear God,
I find a new day dawning
    with blue skies and bright sun.
Let me live it happily.
Let me remember your love for me
    and for your children everywhere. Amen.

—Arlene M. Mark

## 179 Prayer of Thanksgiving

Lord God, Father of us all,
we thank you for the time of harvest;
    for corn and beans,
    for peaches and apples,
    for wheat and oats
    to make our bread and feed our cattle.
We thank you for those who plowed the fields,
    sowed the seed, and gathered in the harvest.
We thank you for things to share,
    for food and joy and friendship
    to make our world a happy place. Amen.

—Arlene M. Mark

## 180 Prayer of Thanksgiving

Loving and creative God,
we thank you for the blessings
    that children bring into this world:
        for their energy and spontaneity,
        for their giggles and laughter,
        for their creative imagination,
        for their sense of freedom and playfulness,
        for their love so openly given,

for their ability to make us feel needed,
for their gift of hope for the future.
Bless the children of this world
and make us like them. Amen.

—Vienna Cobb Anderson, *Prayers of Our Hearts: In Word and Action* (New York:
Crossroad, 1991), 34-35 (adapted)

## Petition and Intercession

**181** **Prayer of Petition**

God of peace,
Bless us with your peace
that we may live together in gentleness and humility.
God of patience,
Bless us with your patience
that we may endure in the time of trial.
God of mercy,
Bless us with your mercy
that we may be pardoned when we have done wrong.
God of strength,
Bless us with your strength
that we may stand firm in time of distress,
through Jesus Christ we pray. Amen.

—Bernhard Albrecht, in *Manual of Worship and Polity* (Brethren Press, 1955), 221
(prayer copyright holder unknown)

## 182 Prayer for the Church

God our Father,
   you intend us to be the body of Jesus Christ, your Son.
You expect us to be
   a voice to speak for him,
   hands to work for him,
   feet to go for him.
Without your help the church can never be
   what you mean it to be.
Cleanse the church
   from all bitterness that would disturb fellowship;
   from all divisions that would destroy unity;
   from all coldness that would lessen devotion;
   from all lethargy that would paralyze purpose.
Defend the church
   from all persecution and attack from without;
   from all heresy and false doctrine from within;
   from enemies who would do it harm;
   from the failure of members to do it good.
Assist and strengthen your church
   with courage in its pronouncements;
   with faithfulness in its witness;
   with conviction in its purpose.
Provide ministers
   whose minds are always learning;
   whose lips speak truth in love;
   whose hearts are full of devotion;
   whose words provide wise counsel;
   whose spirits are caring and brave.
Equip us to be
   generous in giving; faithful in prayer;
   diligent in worship; Christlike in witness;
   patient in disagreement; forbearing and forgiving.

Preserved by your help and goodness, grant that the church
    may indeed be the body of Jesus Christ
        here on earth until he returns. Amen.

—William Barclay, *Prayers for the Christian Year* (London: SCM Press, 1964), 120

# 183   Prayer for Guidance

Shepherd of straying sheep, faithful seeker of the lost,
    watch over your lambs.
Guide us gently by your Shepherd's touch;
    direct us firmly with your staff.

Feed us from your abundant table;
    refresh us at streams of living water;
    embrace us close to your bosom
    and pour oil on our wounds.

Protect us in danger; rescue us when we wander;
    search for the strays; guide the aimless.

In your presence is joy forevermore;
    in your care is life abundant;
    in your keeping is rest and repose;
    in your path is peace.

Shepherd of straying sheep,
    faithful seeker of the lost,
    we will listen for your voice,
    we will answer your call,
    we will trust your righteousness
    and live in your house forevermore. Amen.

—Arlene M. Mark. Based on Ps. 23; Luke 15:3-7

# 184 Prayer for Peace

O Lord, grant that we may not be conformed to the world,
   but may love it and serve in it.
Grant that we may never shrink from being
      the instruments of Thy peace
      because of the judgment of the world.
Grant that we may love Thee without fear of the world.
Grant that we may never believe
      that the inexpressible majesty of Thyself
      may be found in any power of this earth.
May we firstly love Thee and our neighbors as ourselves.
May we remember the poor and the prisoner
      and the sick and the lonely,
      and the young searchers, and the tramps and vagabonds,
      and the lost and the lonely,
      as we remember Christ, who is in them all.
And may we this coming day be able
      to do some work of peace for Thee. Amen.

—Alan Paton, *Instrument of Thy Peace* (copyright © 1968, 1982 by the Seabury
   Press, Inc.; reprinted by permission of HarperCollins Publishers, Inc.; may not
   be reproduced without permission of HarperCollins)

# 185 Prayer Against Violence

Lord Jesus Christ,
we thank you that through your death on the cross
      you disarmed the powers of evil.
Help us, we pray, to enter into your victory
      and to take a stand in your authority against all evil.
Send forth your light and your truth, O Lord.
Bring to light the deeds of darkness,
      and let the plans of violence and murder be defeated.
By the power of your Holy Spirit
      win over those who have allowed their minds
      to be dominated by evil.

Lead them, O Lord, to true repentance
    that they may receive your new life
    and rejoice in your forgiving love. Amen.

—Cecil Kerr, Christian Renewal Centre, Rostrevor, Northern Ireland

# 186  Prayer of Intercession

Most holy and gracious God,
    we praise you for the glorious freedom
    we have together in Christ Jesus.
You have called us to be brothers and sisters
    in the covenant of your church.
Hear our desire to live in covenant relationships
    of binding and loosing,
    so that we may truly be your faithful people.
Enlarge our understandings of how we can be
    "barn raisers" in this technological age.
Forgive us for not being sensitive to one another
    and for preferring a loner pattern of decision making.
As you have forgiven us, may we forgive one another.
May our love flow to each other,
    making our baptismal vows a daily reality.
Hear our prayer for Jesus' sake. Amen.

—Emma Richards, Villa Park, Ill. (adapted). Based on Matt. 6:14; 18:18

# 187  Prayer for the Governments

O Lord, our God,
    we pray for the governments and rulers of the nations.
Do not permit them to shed innocent blood,
    but inspire them to rule according to your will
    as you intend for them to do.
May they promote the good and repress the evil,
    so that we who fear your name

may lead quiet and peaceful lives here on earth.
Give leaders the spirit of wisdom and justice.
Let all who exercise authority
    remember that they have over them a God in heaven;
Let them not pervert power
    which you have delegated unto them,
    and may they be a blessing to the nation.
May we respect and obey the laws,
    that right and good may be promoted.
Let us live peaceably with each other,
    respecting one another,
    and serving God faithfully and in love. Amen.

—*Die ernsthafte Christenpflicht* (original, 1739; HP, 1991), 45; trans. in *A Devoted Christian's Prayer Book* (Aylmer, Ont.: Pathway, 1984), 23, 43 (adapted)

## 188  Prayer for Leaders

Almighty God, have mercy on the people of this land.
Forgive our hardness of heart,
    and contempt of your word and commandments.
Help us to lay aside the pride which deludes us,
    the prejudice which blinds us,
    and the hatred which destroys us.

Lord, give to our leaders patience and wisdom
    and the humility to seek your way forward.
May your Spirit of truth guide them,
    your justice direct them, and your love unite them,
    so that your will may be done.
Through Jesus Christ our Lord. Amen.

—Cecil Kerr, Christian Renewal Centre, Rostrevor, Northern Ireland

# 189 Prayer for Unity

O God, our Father,
for whom the whole family
 in heaven and earth is named,
draw near to us
 that we may truly draw near to one another,
 acknowledging our common humanity,
 confessing our sins to one another and to you,
who alone can keep us
 in the unity of the Spirit
 and the bonds of peace,
 through Jesus Christ our Lord. Amen.

—Joseph E. McCabe, in *Service Book for Ministers* (© 1961 by the author)

# 190 Prayer on Aging

O Keeper of the Seasons,
 through advancing age and gray hair,
You promised to be with us.
We call on you now to keep your promise
 into everlasting life.
Lift us up on eagle's wings,
 give us strength and wisdom,
 the gentleness of a child,
 the ability to be ourselves.
From our first until our final breath,
 your Spirit breathes within us.
From your womb we came,
 and to your womb we gratefully return.
Be with us, in us, and proclaim through us
 our faith in all your promises,
 now and forever. Amen.

—Miriam T. Winter, *WomanWisdom* (New York: Crossroad, 1991), 134 (adapted)

# 191 Prooyer for Freedom

*All: Liberate us, Free Spirit,*
*from all within us that holds us captive.*
*Call us into freedom:*

1: freedom to be
and become and belong;

*2: freedom to stand*
*and admit we were wrong;*

1: freedom to see
and to say what we know;

*2: freedom to fail*
*and freedom to grow;*

1: freedom to feel
and be grateful for feeling;

*2: freedom to heal*
*and to help with our healing;*

1: freedom to laugh
and freedom to cry;

*2: and perhaps above all,*
*the freedom to try.*

*All: Free us, Liberating Spirit,*
*from all around us that holds us captive.*
*Give us freedom*
*for you to be you*
*and me to be me.*
*Come, Spirit of Freedom.*
*Come, set us free.*

—Miriam T. Winter, *WomanWisdom* (New York: Crossroad, 1991), 122
(adapted)

# 192 Prayer for Disciples

Lord of our lives,
we have decided to follow Jesus
and have chosen to be in your kingdom.

Being disciples calls for courage,
>discernment, and unwavering faith.
When we are uncertain, reveal a vision;
when we are passive, light a fire;
when we are tempted, send your Spirit.
Enfold us in your love,
>wrap us about with assurance,
>and infuse us with determination.
Then we can be true disciples,
>and all the world may see
>that we love you.

—Arlene M. Mark

# 193 Petition for the Brothers and Sisters

Heavenly Father,
we pray for all our brothers and sisters in the faith,
>wherever they may be, even unto the ends of the earth,
>whether assembled or scattered, in sorrow or sickness,
>in bonds or in prison for your name's sake.

Comfort them and us with your great love,
>and keep them and us with your Holy Spirit
>and in your word and your will.

May we all abide in your love
>and not depart from the way of righteousness,
>neither to the right nor the left,
>but remain faithful unto the end of our lives.

In Jesus' holy name. Amen.

—*Die ernsthafte Christenpflicht* (original, 1739; HP, 1991), 36; trans. in *A Devoted Christian's Prayer Book* (Aylmer, Ont.: Pathway, 1984), 22-23 (adapted)

# 194 Prayer for Rhythm of Community

L: Lord, we come before you,
　　not alone,
　　but in the company of one another.

**P: We share our happiness with each other,
　　and it becomes greater.**

L: We share our troubles with each other,
　　and they become smaller.

**P: We share one another's griefs and burdens,
　　and their weight becomes possible to bear.**

L: May we never be too mean to give,
　　nor too proud to receive.

**P: For in giving and receiving,
　　we learn to love and be loved;
　　we encounter the meaning of life,
　　the mystery of existence—
　　and discover you. Amen.**

—Terry Falla, in *Be Our Freedom, Lord,* ed. by Terry Falla (Adelaide: Lutheran
　Publishing House, 1984), 158

# 195 Prayer of the People

L: O God, our salvation, you are near to all who call,
**P: hear and answer our prayer.**
L: You are a refuge for the oppressed;
**P: be our stronghold in troubled times.**
L: You set the lonely in families;
**P: do not abandon the parentless.**
L: You stand at the right hand of the needy;
**P: rescue all who are wrongfully condemned.**
L: You raise the poor from the dust;
**P: restore dignity to the outcasts and refugees.**
L: You give food to the hungry;
**P: uphold the cause of the destitute.**
L: You watch over aliens and sustain the widow;
**P: provide protection when there is danger.**

L: You heal the brokenhearted;
**P: bind up the wounds of all who suffer.**
L: You are a mighty God who loves justice;
**P: establish your equity for all humanity.**
L: Praise be to you, O Lord;
**P: you hear and answer our prayer.**

—Karen Moshier Shenk, Harrisonburg, Va.; and Rebecca J. Slough, Richmond, Ind.; in MPH Bulletin, 10-13-85 (adapted)

## 196 Anabaptist Prayer

O my God,
how does it happen in this poor old world,
that you are so great
    yet nobody finds you,
that you call so loudly
    and yet nobody hears you,
that you are so near
    and yet nobody feels you,
that you give yourself to everybody
    and yet nobody knows your name?
We flee from you
    and say we cannot see you;
we turn our backs
    and say we cannot see you;
we stop our ears
    and say we cannot hear you.
Open us to know you
    with all our being. Amen.

—Hans Denck (16th century), in *The Oxford Book of Prayer*, ed. by George Appleton (New York: Oxford Univ. Press, 1985), no. 190 (adapted)

# 197 A Prayer for Nonconformity

L: O holy God,
    you have called us to be nonconformed to this world.
    We pray that we may be saved from adjusting ourselves
        to the world instead of resisting it.

**P: We ask to be forgiven—**
**when we have esteemed the praise of others**
**more than the favor of God;**
**when we have worked with an eye**
**to applause and acceptance by society;**
**when we have reckoned success by worldly standards.**

L: Reunite us with Christ,
    who loved the world and yet never succumbed to it,
    whose love was a revolt
    against all that was ordinary and conformist,
    who blazed a trail for us.

**P: We commit ourselves anew**
**to the standards and values of the kingdom of God.**
**We offer ourselves**
**as instruments and agents of that kingdom.**

L: Help us to be transformers of thought,
    boldly carrying the mind of Christ.

**P: Make us transformers of judgment,**
**giving others a new standard through Jesus Christ.**

L: We pray that Christ might be born in us,
    displacing the old life of selfishness and fear
    with his life of confident joy.

*All: We pray for the renewing of our minds,*
*that we might have that mind in us*
*which was also in Christ Jesus,*

> *so that we may discern what is the will of God,*
> *what is good and acceptable and perfect.*
> *In Jesus' name. Amen.*

—W. B. J. Martin, *Acts of Worship* (Nashville: Abingdon, 1960), 114 (adapted).
Based on Rom. 12:1-2

# 198 Prayer for Love

Christ our teacher, you urge us beyond all reason
    to love our enemies, and pray for our oppressors.
May we embrace such folly
    not through subservience, but strength;
    not through fear, but freedom;
Let us be your witnesses of forgiveness,
    as you have forgiven us, through Jesus Christ. Amen.

—Janet Morley, *All Desires Known* (Wilton, Conn.: Morehouse-Barlow, 1989), 21
(adapted)

# 199 Prayer for Courage

Our God, we would see Jesus as
    the cherished babe lying on the hay,
    the energetic healer of Galilee,
    the triumphant risen Christ.
We confess that we find it troubling
    to speak of Jesus as the humble servant,
    calling us to take up a cross.
We hesitate when loyalty to Jesus
    means discomfort, inconvenience, suffering, or death.
Forgive our too-easy affirmations;
    our noble Sunday-morning intentions
    which quickly slide into weekday compromises.
Nurture us in the eagerness of children,
    the boldness of prophets,
    the vision of poets,

the courage of disciples.
May we continue to trust your promise of a time of peace,
    when swords will be beaten into plowshares,
    when you will wipe away all tears,
    when pain and death will be no more.
May we give our lives in service to that vision,
    living with and for others
    as if the promise were already fulfilled. Amen

—Adapted from Kenneth L. Gibble, in *For All Who Minister* (copyright © 1993,
    Brethren Press, Elgin, Ill.; used by permission)

# 200 Prayer for Service

Lord, make us worthy to serve our fellow people
    who live and die in poverty or hunger around the world.
Through our hands give them this day their daily bread,
    and by our understanding love, give peace and joy.

—Mother Teresa, Calcutta, in *The Oxford Book of Prayer*, ed. by George Appleton
    (New York: Oxford Univ. Press, 1985), no. 219 (adapted)

# 201 Prayer for Families

God of eternal love,
we thank you for the sense of belonging
    and the nurturing we enjoy from family life.
We learn to love, to share and care,
    to be strong and gentle, to give and receive.
Forgive us when we are self-focused
    to the exclusion of the other's good.
Forgive us when we are short of courtesy,
    consideration, and kindness.
May our love be patient, thoughtful, and generous.
Help us to carry each other's burdens
    and share every goodness, always reflecting your love.
Give us strength to serve each other,

wisdom to respect our differences,
and grace to offer words and deeds
that build us up together in your righteousness. Amen.

—Arlene M. Mark

# 202  Prayer

Help me, O God,
to believe that whatever it is
    I want or need,
I ought to tell you about it;
and I ought also to believe
    that you will answer my prayer,
    even though your answer may be different
    from the one I hope for.
So shall I be
    your loving and trusting child,
and all things will work together for good.

—Donald O. Soper, *Children's Prayer Time* (Epworth Press; adapted). Based on
  Rom. 8:28

# 203  Prayer for Social Justice

Creator of us all,
your human children are one family in you,
    so that what concerns any must concern all.
We confess our dulled awareness
    that does not know what others suffer.
We have been guilty of selfishness and strife
    when we should be working for unity and fellowship.
We have been content that we should prosper
    though many are poor,
    that a few should feast
    while multitudes are famished in body and soul.

Creator of us all,
you have taught us that
    whatsoever we sow, we shall also reap.
Help us to repent.
Call us to your redemptive purposes.
Work through us to build
    a new and better order on this earth.
Creator of us all,
    may your name be glorified
    and all your children be blessed. Amen.

—Adapted from *Lift Up Your Hearts* by Walter Russell Bowie (copyright renewal
  © 1984 by Mrs. Jean B. Evans, Mrs. Elizabeth Chapman, and Mrs. Walter
  Russell Bowie, Jr.; used by permission of the publisher, Abingdon Press)

# 204 Prayer

Heavenly Father, hear our prayer.
    Keep us in your loving care.
Guard us through the livelong day,
    in our work and in our play.
Keep us pure and kind and true
    in everything we say and do. Amen.

—*A Little Book of Prayers and Graces*, ed. by Quail Hawkins (New York: Doubleday, 1941; adapted)

# 205 Bidding Prayer

Faithful God, Lord of all, we offer our prayers to you
    for a world in need.
Let us pray for the church worldwide. *(pause)*
    Lord of the church, give us unity in the Spirit,
    to be one in the witness of saving love,
    and with one mind and one mouth to glorify you.
Let us pray for our congregation. *(pause)*
Head of the body,

give us wisdom to follow your commandments,
to live peacefully, to do justly,
and to walk humbly with you.
Let us pray for those in power. *(pause)*
Creator and ruler of the universe,
give to all who exercise authority and determine destiny,
wisdom and virtue to bless your people
and bring peace across the land.
Let us pray for the anguished in body and soul. *(pause)*
Source of all compassion, give to all who suffer,
the light of your presence and the caring of your people,
to bring calm and comfort.
Let us pray for our enemies. *(pause)*
Giver of good to all, take from us any evil thought or will
so that we may forgive those who offend us
as you have forgiven us
and bring them to your saving grace.
Let us pray for ourselves. *(pause)*
All-knowing One, you who see us as we are
and know us as we should be,
forgive our sins, set us free from fear,
and give us life abundant with your guiding presence,
that we may be yours forever,
through Jesus Christ our Lord. Amen.

—Arlene M. Mark

# 206 Bidding Prayer

Holy Lord, we acclaim you glorious in power.
From everlasting to everlasting, you are our God.
To you we bring our praise and our supplications.

We pray for your church universal,
that it may be an unfaltering witness,
a light in darkness, and salt in a tasteless world. *(pause)*

We pray for each one who has confessed your name,
    that we may truly and humbly serve you
    and bring glory to your name. *(pause)*
We pray for peace in our world,
    understanding that promotes peace
    and unites all people in love. *(pause)*
We pray for those who lead our nations,
    that they may have courage, honor, and wisdom
    to rule for peace and justice for all. *(pause)*
We pray for those who suffer pain, grief, or trouble,
    that they may know the assurance of your presence
    and trust in you to provide. *(pause)*
We pray for the mission of the church,
    that everywhere its faithful witness
    may invite those who do not yet believe,
    to know and follow Christ. *(pause)*
We pray for ourselves, for the forgiveness of our sins,
    that freed from any weight or fear,
    we may serve you with an abundance of joy
    and honor you fully. *(pause)*
Holy Lord, hear and answer our prayer,
    that we may rest in your assurance
    to hear our supplications,
    for yours is the kingdom, the power, and the glory,
        now and forevermore. Amen.

—Arlene M. Mark. Based on prayers in *Book of Common Prayer According to the Use of the Episcopal Church* (New York: The Church Hymnal Corp., 1979)

# Offering Invitations and Prayers

## 207 Offertory Invitation

L: Give to the Lord the glory due his name;
　　bring an offering and come before him.
**P: We will sacrifice a thank offering to God**
　　**and call on the name of the Lord.**
**We will fulfill our vows to the Lord,**
　　**in the presence of all God's people.**
L: Let each of us use whatever gift we have received,
　　faithfully sharing God's grace in many forms.
**P: Freely we have received; freely we will give.**

—Arlene M. Mark. Based on 1 Chron. 16:29; Ps. 116:17-18; 1 Pet. 4:10; Matt.
10:8b

## 208 Offertory Invitation

God has shown us the meaning of generosity
　　in the beautiful diversity of creation,
　　in the overflowing love of Jesus Christ,
　　in the never-ending gift of the Holy Spirit.
God has abundantly blessed us and called us
　　to be a community that honors each other,
　　to be servants to others with joy,
　　to share our love and material possessions.
Let us rejoice in what we have been given
　　and in what is ours to give.

—Ann B. Day, in *Touch Holiness*, ed. Ruth C. Duck and Maren C. Tirabassi
(Cleveland: Pilgrim Press, 1990) 213 (adapted)

## 209 Offering Invitation

No one gives oneself freely and willingly
    to God's service unless,
    having tasted the Father's love,
    that one is drawn in love
    and worship God in return.

—John Calvin (16th century). Reprinted from *Prayers of the Reformers,* ed. by Clyde Manschreck (copyright © 1958 Muhlenberg Press; used by permission of Augsburg Fortress; may not be reproduced without permission of Augsburg Fortress)

## 210 Offertory Invitation

The willingness to give is a sign of life.
The fruit tree gives of its fruit,
    and we know it is alive.
When it no longer gives,
    we know real life has gone out of it.
The heart that hoards the blessings of God
    is no longer alive with spiritual power.
To give is to live.

—Adapted from Earl W. Fike, Jr., in *For All Who Minister* (copyright © 1993, Brethren Press, Elgin, Ill.; used by permission)

## 211 Offering Invitation

Truly God is good to us in ways beyond our understanding.
We ponder not how much we shall give,
    but how much we shall withhold.
Our God says,
    "The world and all that is in it is mine."
Our God owns the cattle on a thousand hills.

Yet those who bring thanksgiving as their sacrifice,
    bring honor to God.
In humble gratitude, let us present our thanks to God.

—Arlene M. Mark. Based on Ps. 50:7-15, 23

# 212 Offering Invitation

Christ has taught us that we cannot love both God and wealth.
Our hearts will always be focused first on our riches.
Let us be faithful stewards
    of our time, our talents, and our money,
so that our treasure is in heaven
    and our giving pleases God.

—Arlene M. Mark. Based on Matt. 6:19-24; 25:14-30; Luke 12:34

# 213 Offering Invitation

Jesus told the story of a man
    who had a rich return on his investment.
He said to himself, "Lucky man!
    You have all you need for many years.
    Enjoy the security of your years of labor."
That man lost his barns, his profits, and his soul.
Let us be careful that our riches do not cost us our salvation.

—Arlene M. Mark. Based on Luke 12:16-21

# 214 Offertory Invitations

1. No one should appear before the Lord empty-handed;
       all should give as they are able,
           according to the blessing of the Lord your God
           that has been given you. *(based on Deut. 16:16b-17)*

2. Ascribe to the Lord the glory due his name;
       bring an offering, and come into his courts.
   Worship the Lord in holy splendor;
       tremble before him, all the earth. *(Ps. 96:8-9)*

3. L: Bless the Lord, O my soul,
       and all that is within me, bless God's holy name.
   **P: Bless the Lord, O my soul,**
       **and do not forget all his benefits.** *(based on Ps. 103:1-?)*

4. What shall I return to the Lord
       for all his bounty to me?
   I will give what I have promised
       in the presence of all God's people. *(based on Ps. 116:12, 14)*

5. Honor the Lord with your substance
       and with the first fruits of all your produce.
   Do not withhold good from those to whom it is due,
       when it is in your power to do it. *(Prov. 3:9, 27)*

6. A generous person will be enriched,
       and one who gives water will get water.
   Those who trust in their riches will wither,
       but the righteous will flourish
       like green leaves. *(Prov. 11:25, 28)*

7. Some pretend to be rich, yet have nothing;
       others pretend to be poor, yet have great wealth.
   Some give freely, yet grow all the richer;
       others withhold what is due,
       and only suffer want. *(Prov. 13:7; 11:24)*

8. Whoever is kind to the poor
       lends to the Lord, and will be repaid in full.
   Those who are generous are blessed,
       for they share their bread with the poor. *(Prov. 19:17; 22:9)*

9. Bring the full tithe into the storehouse,
       so that there may be food in my house,
   and thus put me to the test, says the Lord of hosts;
       see if I will not open the windows of heaven for you

and pour down for you an overflowing blessing. *(Mal. 3:10)*

10. Do not store up for yourselves treasures on earth,
    where moth and rust consume
    and where thieves break in and steal;
    but store up for yourselves treasures in heaven,
    where neither moth nor rust consumes
    and where thieves do not break in and steal.
    For where your treasure is,
    there your heart will be also. *(Matt. 6:19-21)*

11. The one who sows sparingly will also reap sparingly,
    and the one who sows bountifully will also reap bountifully.
    Each of us must give as we have made up our mind,
    not reluctantly or under compulsion,
    for God loves a cheerful giver.
    And God is able to provide us
    with every blessing in abundance
    so we may share abundantly in every good work.
    We will be enriched in every way for our great generosity,
    which will produce thanksgiving to God through us.
    *(based on 2 Cor. 9:6-11)*

12. How does God's love abide in anyone
    who has the world's goods
    and sees a brother or sister in need
    and yet refuses to help?
    Dear children, let us love,
    not only in word or speech,
    but also in truth and action. *(based on 1 John 3:17-18)*

13. God has been good to us in ways we do not understand
    and for reasons we cannot comprehend.
    Let us honor God with our gifts,
    out of thankful hearts and joyous spirits. *(Arlene M. Mark)*

14. Christ has taught us it is more blessed to give than to receive.
    Let us present our offerings
    to the service of the church,
    and commit them to God's blessing
    for those who give and those who receive.

    *(Arlene M. Mark)*

15. Let us give thanks to the Lord
    with all our being.
    In the company of the upright,
    let us honor God for the blessings
    and goodness we have received. *(based on Ps. 111:1)*

# 215 Blessing and Protest

If you share your bread in fear,
    mistrustingly, undaringly,
in a trice your bread will fail.
Try sharing it without looking ahead,
    not thinking of the cost, unstintingly,
like a child of the Lord of all the harvests in the world.

—Helder Camara, in *Be Our Freedom, Lord,* ed. by Terry Falla, 2d ed. (Adelaide: Open Book Publishers, 1994), 193

# 216 Offertory Prayer

"Toiling, one must help the weak,
remembering the words of the Lord Jesus, when he said,
'There is more happiness in giving than in receiving.' "
**Almighty God, there is no doubt**
**about the adequacy of our receiving.**
Let there be no doubt about the generosity of our giving.
**Accept our offering, through Jesus Christ our Lord. Amen.**

—Ronald N. Ham, in *Be Our Freedom, Lord,* ed. by Terry Falla (Adelaide: Lutheran Publishing House, 1984), 159. Based on Acts 20:35

# 217 Offertory Prayer

God of extravagant mercy,
>with hands outstretched you have poured out
>wonder and pleasure and delight,
>goodness and beauty and bounty.

So take these offerings, we pray, as our protest against all
>that is evil and ugly and impoverished,
>trivial and wretched and tyrannical,
>in our world and ourselves—

And thus may we and others know
>ourselves to be blessed. Amen.

—Terry Falla and Beryl Turner, in *Be Our Freedom, Lord,* ed. by Terry Falla, 2d ed. (Adelaide: Open Book Publishers, 1994)

# 218 Offertory Prayer

Gracious God, we give our best,
>lest in gaining the world we lose life itself.

As a covenant people, we seek to witness to your will and way.

Help us to know more clearly what you would have us do
>with the wealth entrusted to our care.

As we contribute to the needs of the saints,
>we present ourselves as living sacrifices.

Direct us according to your will. Amen.

—LaVon Bayler, *Fresh Winds of the Spirit*, book 2: *Liturgical Resources for Year A* (Cleveland: Pilgrim Press, 1992), 125 (adapted). Based on Rom. 12:1-13

# 219 Offertory Prayer

L: Yours, Lord, is the greatness,
>the power and the glory,
>the victory and the majesty.

P: **All that is in the heavens
and in the earth is yours,
and you rule over all.**
L: Therefore, Lord, receive these offerings,
our tangible expressions of love and gratitude.
P: **Touch them into life for many,
so that your kingdom may grow
in the hearts of all.
In the name of Jesus. Amen.**

—Ronald N. Ham, in *Be Our Freedom, Lord,* ed. by Terry Falla (Adelaide: Lutheran Publishing House, 1984), 160

# 220 Offertory Responsive

L: Ever-giving God,
source of all goodness and charity,
your ear is always open to our needs.
P: **When we cry to you,
you are faithful and provide for us.**
L: In gratitude, we bring our thanksgiving.
P: **For all your mercies,
we return to you from our abundance.**
L: All that we give, we dedicate to your glory.
P: **All that we keep, we commit to your care,
for we are only stewards of your bounty.
Bless what we give and what we keep,
for all is your creation. Amen.**

—Arlene M. Mark

# 221 Offertory Prayer

Lord, we bring before you
 the common things of our common life:
 our money, our songs,
 our labors to be your faithful congregation,
 our needs and dreams,
 our joys and sorrows,
 our selves.
We celebrate all this with you,
 seeking the touch of your Spirit
 so that we will share more deeply
 what we are and have
 with all our brothers and sisters
 in our city and our world.
In faith and gratitude we offer common things
 made miracles by your grace. Amen.

—Source unknown

# 222 Offertory Prayer

Generous God, you have given us life,
 a place to live in,
 and people to live with.
Open our eyes to each other
 and to all our brothers and sisters,
 especially the poor, the oppressed, the alienated.
Make us humble enough to help and comfort them,
 so that a little of your love and justice and peace
 may come to this place.
We make bold to consecrate ourselves and our gifts
 to you and the service of others,
 through Jesus Christ our Lord. Amen.

—Source unknown; adapted by Theodore W. Loder, Germantown, Pa.

## 223 Offering

All things come from you, O God,
>and with gratitude we return to you what is yours.

You created all that is,
>and with love formed us in your image.

You gave your only Son Jesus Christ to be our Savior.

All that we are, and all that we have, is a trust from you.

And so, in gratitude for all your gifts,
>we offer you ourselves, and all that we have,
>in union with Christ's offering for us.

By your Holy Spirit make us one with Christ,
>one with each other, and one in ministry to all the world;
>through Jesus Christ our Savior. Amen.

—Hoyt L. Hickman, from "The Worship Resources" of *The United Methodist Hymnal* (© 1989 UMPH; used by permission), 51 (adapted)

## 224 Offering

Generous God, you are the owner of the universe.

We have nothing we can bring
>that would make you richer or better
>or obligate you to us.

All we have comes to us from you,
>the giver of all good things.

But we bring this offering as our gift today
>to dramatize our thankfulness to you.

In giving, we also support our church,
>so that we may carry on the tasks
>we have jointly decided to do
>in our community and our world.

Accept our thanks and our gifts
>as expressions of our love. Amen.

—Fred Unruh, in *Prayers for Public Worship*, ed. by Edward K. Ziegler (Elgin, Ill.: Brethren Press, 1986), 20 (adapted)

# 225 Offertory

Giver of all gifts,
you open your hand
    and satisfy the desire of every living thing.
You are just in all your ways
    and kind in all your doings.
Teach us to give freely
    as you have given.
Teach us to live thankfully
    in ministry to others.
Bless the givers with joy
    and the receivers with gratitude,
    so that your name may be blessed. Amen.

—Arlene M. Mark. Based on Ps. 145:16-17

# 226 Gifts Are for Using

God of Jesus, Father of us all,
    with these gifts we offer you our lives
    to do your work in the world.
Take our bodies and our minds,
    **our work and our leisure,**
Our relationships with other people,
    **our friendships and our family life,**
Our dreams and our doubts,
    **Our faith and our plans for the future.**
In the name of Christ Jesus our Lord,
    **we bring them to you. Amen.**

—Terry Falla, in *Be Our Freedom, Lord,* ed. by Terry Falla, 2d ed. (Adelaide: Open Book Publishers, 1994), 197

# Sending

## 227 Benediction

We praise you, O God,
>for being with us
>in this special time and place.

Send us forth
>with courage to be witnesses
>of your work in the world.

Let us not forget your name or power;
>let us not miss your glory in the mundane;
>let us not trample on holy ground,
>through Christ we pray. Amen.

—Jennifer Halteman Schrock, Columbus, Ohio (adapted)

## 228 Benediction

Hallelujah! Hallelujah!

May the God-Who-Has-Come anoint you with power
>to be ambassadors of peace in the name of Christ!

Blest be the name of the Lord! Amen.

—Philip K. Clemens, Goshen, Ind. (adapted; the *hallelujahs* may follow a hymn of
rejoicing but could be omitted if not suitable)

## 229 Benediction

May the Spirit of the Lord anoint you to provide
>strength to the weak,
>freedom to the oppressed,
>food to the hungry,
>and good news to the poor.

Blest be the name of the Lord! Amen.

—Philip K. Clemens, Goshen, Ind.

# 230 Responsive Benediction

L: I pray that you, being rooted and established in love,
    may have power, together with all the saints,
    to grasp how wide and long and high and deep
      is the love of Christ.
    And to know this love that surpasses knowledge—
    that you may be filled to the measure
      of all the fullness of God.

*All: Now to God who is able to do immeasurably more*
    *than all we ask or imagine,*
    *according to his power that is at work within us,*
    *to him be glory in the church and in Christ Jesus*
    *throughout all generations, forever and ever. Amen.*

—Eph. 3:17b-21, NIV

# 231 Benediction

God, whose breath gave life and being,
    bless you this day with joy and goodness.

God, whose Son brought salvation and life eternal,
    bless you this day with grace and newness of soul.

God, whose Spirit empowers with vision and understanding,
    bless you this day with courage and wisdom.

God bless you, now and forever. Amen.

—Arlene M. Mark

# 232 Closing

L: As we leave this time of worship,
    we take along our "Yes!" to God.

1: Yes! We will be lit candles of love
    against the darkness of hate.

2: Yes! We will be joyful songs,
   filling the silence of indifference.

1: Yes! We will be a hopeful community
   in a discouraged world.

2: Yes! We will bring life
   to people surrounded by death.

All: *For we are people of love, of joy, of hope, of life.*
   *We follow the Prince of Peace,*
   *and we carry his peace with us*
      *as we go into the world.*

L: Excited by the possibilities of peace,
   all the people of God shouted,

All: *Yes!*

L: Then, knowing they were not sure
      what they had committed to,
   the followers of the Prince of Peace,
      who live with the indwelling Spirit,
      whispered in awe,

All: *Amen, so be it!*

L: Now go forth
      to live your Yes! to God,
   knowing that you are held by a love
      that will not let you go.

   In the name of the Creator, the Redeemer,
      and the Sustainer. Amen.

—Susan Mark Landis in Peace-Justice-Service Commission Bulletin, 10-13-91,
Ohio Mennonite Conference, Berlin, Ohio

# 233 Benediction

God sends us into the world,
    to accept the cost
    and to discover the joy
    of discipleship.
Therefore go—
    carrying with you
    the peace of Christ,
    the love of God,
    and the encouragement of the Holy Spirit,
    in trial and rejoicing. Amen.

—Ruth C. Duck, *Bread for the Journey: Resources for Worship Based on the New Ecumenical Lectionary* (Cleveland: Pilgrim Press, 1981), 70

# 234 Benediction

Lord, take our minds
    and think through them.
Take our lips
    and speak through them.
Take our hearts
    and set them on fire.

—Source unknown; supplied through William Sloane Coffin

# 235 Prayer

Eternal God, lead me now
    out of the familiar setting of my doubts and fears,
    beyond my pride and my need to be secure,
    into a strange and graceful ease
    with my true proportions and with yours;

that in boundless silence,
>I may grow strong enough to endure
>and flexible enough to share your grace,
>through Jesus Christ our guide. Amen.

—Exerpted from the book *Guerrillas of Grace*, by Ted Loder (copyright © 1984 by LuraMedia; reprinted by permission of LuraMedia, Inc., San Diego)

# 236 Benediction

The grace of our Lord Jesus Christ be with you.
Be at peace.
Always seek to do good to one another
>and to all.
Rejoice always, pray without ceasing.
>Give thanks in all circumstances.
Hold fast to what is good.
May the God of peace sanctify you entirely,
>and may your spirit and soul and body
>be kept sound and blameless
>at the coming of our Lord Jesus Christ.

—Arlene M. Mark. Based on 1 Thess. 5:13-28

# 237 Benediction

L: God is light,
*All: and in God there is no darkness at all.*

L: God is light;
*All: let us walk in the light as God himself is in the light.*

L: God is light.
*All: Let us go to be a light to those who are in darkness.*

—Susan Yoder Ackerman, Newport News, Va., in MPH Bulletin, 4-10-94 (adapted). Based on 1 John 1:5, 7; Rom. 2:19

# 238 Sending

L: We came to celebrate God's mysterious ways.
**P: Our God is love.**
L: We remembered God's story of love to us and all humankind.
**P: Our God is love.**
L: We go to share that story in word and deed,
**P: for our God is love.**

—Ken Bechtel, Toronto, in MPH Bulletin, 7-10-94

# 239 Sending

May the seed of Christ's word,
    planted and watered by the Holy Spirit,
    find root and grow in your hearts.
May your work and your relationships
    reflect Christ's constant presence
    in the days of this week. Amen.

—David B. Greiser, Jr., Philadelphia, in MPH Bulletin, 2-14-93. Based on 1 Cor.
    3:7-9

# 240 Sending

L: We go now with faith,
    trusting God's Spirit to guide us;
**P: We go now with hope,**
    **waiting for the fullness of Christ's reign.**
L: We go now with love,
    resting in God's care and the care of God's people.

**All:  We go out with joy:**
        **to listen and speak,**
        **to sing and suffer,**
        **to proclaim good news,**
        **and give glory to God.**

—Marlene Kropf, Elkhart, Ind.

# 241 Benediction

Go into the world and do what the Lord requires:
    living with kindness and justice,
    walking your path humbly, with God.
Then you will find yourselves blessed.

Know that yours is the kingdom of heaven,
    yours the strength and mercy of God,
yours all the blessings given to God's beloved children. Amen.

—Diane Karay, *All the Seasons of Mercy* (© 1987 Diane Karay; used by permission
of Westminster John Knox Press), 132. Based on Mic. 6:8; Matt. 5:1-12

# 242 Benediction

We reaffirm our desire to continue in and witness to
    the simple and nonresistant faith,
    looking for that blessed hope
    and the glorious appearing of our great God
    and Savior, Jesus Christ.

—Franconia Mennonite Conference, traditional commitment at the end of
semiannual conference sessions

# 243 Scripture Benedictions

1. May the God of hope
fill you with all joy and peace in believing,
so that you may abound in hope
by the power of the Holy Spirit. *(Rom. 15:13)*

2. Peace to the brothers and sisters, and love with faith
from God the Father and the Lord Jesus Christ,
Grace to all who love our Lord Jesus Christ
with an undying love. *(based on Eph. 6:23-24, NIV)*

3. Live in peace;
and the God of love and peace will be with you.
The grace of the Lord Jesus Christ,
the love of God,
and the communion of the Holy Spirit
be with all of you. Amen. *(2 Cor. 13:11b, 13)*

4. May the God of steadfastness and encouragement
grant you to live in harmony
with one another,
in accordance with Christ Jesus,
so that together you may with one voice
glorify the God and Father
of our Lord Jesus Christ. *(Rom. 15:5-6)*

5. The Lord watch between you and me,
when we are absent one from the other. *(Gen. 31:49)*

6. The Lord bless you and keep you;
the Lord make his face to shine upon you,
and be gracious to you;
the Lord lift up his countenance upon you
and give you peace. Amen. *(Num. 6:24-26)*

7. The Lord be gracious to us and bless us
   and make his face to shine upon us,
   so that his way may be known upon earth and
   his saving power among all nations. *(based on Ps. 67:1-2*

8. The Lord will keep you from all evil; he will keep your life.
   The Lord will keep your going out and your coming in
   from this time on and forevermore. *(Ps. 121:7-8)*

9. Now may our Lord Jesus Christ and God our Father,
   who loved us and through grace
   gave us eternal comfort and good hope,
   comfort your hearts and strengthen them
   in every good work and word. *(2 Thess. 2:16-17)*

10. May the God of peace sanctify you entirely;
    and may your spirit and soul and body
    be kept sound and blameless
    at the coming of our Lord Jesus Christ. *(1 Thess. 5:23)*

11. The grace of the Lord Jesus Christ, the love of God,
    and the communion of the Holy Spirit
    be with you all. *(2 Cor. 13:13)*

12. The peace of God, which surpasses all understanding,
    will guard your hearts and minds in Christ Jesus. *(Phil. 4:7)*

13. Now to him who is able to keep you from falling,
    and to make you stand without blemish
    in the presence of his glory with rejoicing,
    to the only God our Savior,
    through Jesus Christ our Lord,
    be glory, majesty, power, and authority,
    before all time and forever. Amen. *(Jude 24-25)*

# Ordinances

## Baptism

**244** **Call to Worship**

L: Come to the Christ,
　　through whom we are granted forgiveness of sins
　　and given new and eternal life.

**P: To all who receive him,**
　　**who believe in his name,**
　　**he gives power to become the children of God.**

L: Once we were not a people,
　　but now we are God's people;
　　once we had not received mercy,
　　but now we have received mercy.

**P: When the goodness and loving kindness**
　　**of God our Savior appeared, he saved us,**
　　**not because of any works of righteousness we have done,**
　　**but according to his mercy, through the water of rebirth**
　　**and renewal of the Holy Spirit,**
　　**so that we might become heirs together,**
　　**according to the hope of eternal life.**

—Arlene M. Mark. Based on John 1:12; 1 Pet. 2:10; Titus 3:4-5, 7

# 245 Call to Worship

L: Taste and see that the Lord is good;
    Happy are those who take refuge in him.
**P: The salvation of the righteous is from the Lord;**
    **God is our refuge in the time of trouble.**
L: All we have sinned
    and fall short of the glory of God;
**P: No one can enter the kingdom of God**
    **without being born of water and Spirit.**
*All: Blessed are those who wash their robes;*
    *and are incorporated into God's acts of salvation.*

—Arlene M. Mark. Based on Pss. 34:8; 37:39; Rom. 3:23; John 3:5; Rev. 22:14

# 246 Historic Prayer

Make yourself manifest, O Lord,
    and grant that _____, being baptized,
    may be transformed by putting off the old self,
    corrupted by deceitful lusts;
    and putting on the new self,
    formed fresh according to the image of the Creator.

Grafted through baptism into the likeness of your death,
    may *they/he/she* become a partaker also in thy resurrection.

May *they/he/she* guard the gift of your Holy Spirit,
    may *they/he/she* increase the measure of grace
    which has been entrusted to *them/him/her*,
    and so may *they/he/she* receive the prize
    which is God's calling to life above,
    being numbered among the firstborn,
    whose names are written in heaven. Amen.

—Eastern Orthodox, in *The Oxford Book of Prayer*, ed. by George Appleton (New York: Oxford Univ. Press, 1985), no. 690 (adapted). Based on Eph. 4:22-24, 7; Rom. 6:5; Phil. 3:14

# 247 Anabaptist Prayer for Baptism

Almighty and merciful God,
> you made us for yourself, in your image.
> We rejected you but you kept on loving us.
> Finally, you sent your Son to find us.

You command all who accept your love and grace
> to be baptized in Jesus' name.
> This is the heart's desire of these present before you.

Make them strong to conquer evil;
> in the end, give them the crown of life.
> Help them to say no to false loves.

Make them brothers and sisters of Christ;
> give them the gifts of the Spirit.

To you be glory and to them salvation,
> in Jesus' name. Amen.

—Leenaerdt Clock (1625), trans. by John D. Rempel from *Formulier etlichen
   christlichen Gebäthe* (A formulary of several Christian prayers)

# 248 The Signature of Your Image

Creator God, in whose image we are made
> and whose personal signature is
> written on the very heart of our being:

**Help us to create in this community
> the climate of love and compassion,
> understanding and affirmation,
> that all of us need if we
> are to grow to our
> full promise. Amen.**

—Terry Falla, in *Be Our Freedom, Lord*, ed. by Terry Falla (Adelaide: Open Book
   Publishers, 1994), 197

# 249 Baptism

O Lord, we ask you to send your blessing upon your *servant/s*
　　who today *acknowledge/s* before us the desire
　　to be a follower and friend of Jesus Christ.
Strengthen *them/him/her* by your Spirit,
　　that *they/he/she* may live worthy of the confession
　　which is being made this day.
Give *them/her/him* grace to be *(a)* good *persons/man/woman,*
　　full of the Holy Spirit and of faith.
Give unto *them/him/her* an ever-increasing love for you,
　　for your church, and for your call to discipleship and service.
Guide *them/him/her* in a new ministry of love,
　　born of devotion to Jesus Christ.
When *their/his/her* work is completed on earth,
　　receive *them/him/her* into your eternal kingdom;
　　through Jesus Christ our Lord. Amen.

—*Minister's Service Book,* ed. by J. D. Morrison (adapted; copyright 1937 by Lillett, Clark and Co.; copyright renewed © 1965 by James D. Morrison, Jr.; reprinted by permission of HarperCollins Publishers, Inc.; may not be reproduced or reprinted without permission of HarperCollins)

# 250 Prayer

Holy and gracious God, we thank you for the gift of baptism.
In the waters of baptism we are buried with Christ in his death;
from the water we are raised to share in his resurrection;
through the water we are reborn by the power of the Holy Spirit.
We praise you for claiming us through our baptism
　　and for upholding us by your grace.

By your Holy Spirit renew us,
>    that we may be empowered to do your will,
> and continue forever in the risen life of Christ,
>> to whom, with you and the Holy Spirit,
>> be all glory and honor, now and forever. Amen.

—*Liturgical Year,* Supplemental Liturgical Resource 7 (Louisville: Westminster/
John Knox, © 1992; used by permission of Westminster John Knox Press), 200
(adapted)

## 251 Baptism Prayer

O God, Lord of Life,
>    we praise you that your Spirit has touched our life,
>    that your presence surrounds us even now.
> We speak the words, we do the actions;
>    only you can know the heart;
>    cleanse the soul, seal the commitment.
> Grant now that this act of baptism
>    may establish and strengthen _____
>    and all of us gathered here.
> Grant *them/him/her* joy in new relationships;
>    sustain *them/him/her* as your *children/child;*
>    show your grace in *their/his/her* life.
> We thank you also for the church
>    and for these times of sharing faith and trust with each other,
>    in Jesus' name. Amen.

—Harold Bauman, in *Baptism and Church Membership* (Worship Series, 3), ed. by
James H. Waltner (MPH, 1979), 36 (adapted)

## 252 Baptismal Response

Today you are sealing your confession of commitment to Christ.
In this outward sign of your inward faith,
　　you are initiated as *members/a member* of Christ's church.
We welcome you into our fellowship
　　and pledge with you to commit ourselves to Christ,
　　seeking the guidance and power of the Holy Spirit
　　to die unto self and rise in the resurrection.
We offer you our prayers, our presence,
　　our loving care and counsel,
　　so that we all may lead lives worthy of the Lord,
　　fully pleasing to him.
Together we are united to Christ and to each other,
　　made strong with the strength of his glorious power.
We joyfully thank the Father who has rescued us
　　from the power of darkness
　　and received us into the kingdom of Christ.

—Arlene M. Mark

## 253 Benediction

When we were buried with Christ in baptism,
　　we were also raised with Christ
　　through faith in the power of God,
　　who raised Christ from the dead.

May God bless us
　　to lead lives worthy of the calling
　　to which we have been called.

—Philip K. Clemens, Goshen, Ind. Based on Col. 2:12; Eph. 4:1

# The Lord's Supper and Foot Washing

## 254 Responsive Reading

L: The love of Christ has gathered us as one,
　　　to remember Jesus Christ, the Son of God,
　　　who loved his own until the end.

**P: In his great, unselfish love,**
　　　**the Master who calmed the storms**
　　　**and turned water into wine,**
　　　**stooped to do a servant's duty**
　　　**and washed his disciples' feet.**

L: When we are gathered here,
　　　let us be drawn together by his passion.
　　　Let no pride dismiss his model,
　　　let no love be less than his.

**P: Let us follow Christ's example**
　　　**and demonstrate the service**
　　　**by which we show love for one another.**
　　　**For by this, the world will know**
　　　**that we are Christ's disciples,**
　　　**if we love one another.**

—Arlene M. Mark. Based on John 13:34-35

## 255 Responsive Reading

L: Fellow servants of our Lord Jesus Christ,
　　　let us serve one another as Christ has taught.

**P: On the night he was betrayed,**
　　　**Jesus took a basin and towel,**
　　　**the symbols of servanthood,**
　　　**and kneeling in an act of humility,**
　　　**he washed the feet of those who were his own.**

L: In this way he taught equality
　　　and called all disciples to serve one another.

P:  We stoop to wash each other's feet
and remember Christ's self-giving,
even to the cross.
L:  The memory of Christ's example
calls us to serve one another in love and humility.
P:  Let us serve God through serving one another:
opening our hearts to embrace each other,
rejecting pride and power,
symbolizing our sharing in the body of Christ
so that the mystery of Christ's act
might work its miracle in our lives.

—Arlene M. Mark. Based on John 13

# 256 Prayer

O God,  your love lived in Jesus Christ,
who washed disciples' feet on the night of his betrayal.
Wash from us the stain of sin,
so that, in hours of danger, we may not fail,
but follow your Son through every trial,
and praise him to the world as Lord and Christ,
to whom be glory now and forever. Amen.

—*Liturgical Year,* Supplemental Liturgical Resource 7 (Louisville:
Westminster/John Knox, © 1992), 161, from *The Worshipbook* (Philadelphia:
Westminster, © 1972; used by permission of Westminister John Knox Press)

# 257 Call to Worship

L:   We gather as people of the new covenant
which is sealed with Christ's blood.
P: Praise God for Jesus Christ
who atoned for our sins once and for all.
L:  We celebrate our redemption
as we commune at our Lord's table.

**P: We dedicate this service
to the memory and praise
of our Lord's sacrificial love for us.**

—Phil Bedsworth, Hesston, Kan., in his notebooks

## 258 Prayer for Self-Examination

Almighty God, our minds have so many hidden recesses
    that it is difficult to thoroughly purge them
    from all pretense and lying.
Grant that we may honestly examine ourselves.
Shine upon us with the light of your Holy Spirit.

May we truly acknowledge our hidden faults
    and put them far away from us,
    so that you may be our only God.
May we offer you pure and spotless worship,
    and conduct ourselves in the world with a pure conscience.
May we be so occupied in our duties
    as to seek another's advantage as well as our own.
At length make us partakers of your true glory
    which you have prepared for us in heaven,
    through Christ our Lord. Amen.

—John Calvin (16th century), *Commentary of Daniel.* Reprinted from *Prayers of the
Reformers*, ed. by Clyde Manschreck (copyright © 1958 Muhlenberg Press;
used by permission of Augsburg Fortress; may not be reproduced without
permission of Augsburg Fortress), 153

## 259 Prayer of Confession

Father, we have sinned
    against heaven and before you
    and are not worthy to be called your children.
Only speak a consoling word,
    and our souls will be made whole.

God, be gracious to us sinners.
May the almighty, eternal, and gracious God,
    have mercy on all our sins
    and forgive us graciously,
    and lead us, freed from our faults,
    into eternal life,
    through Jesus Christ our Lord and Savior. Amen.

—Balthasar Hubmaier (1527), in *Balthasar Hubmaier: Theologian of Anabaptism*
(Classics of the Radical Reformation, 5), trans. and ed. by H. Wayne Pipkin and
John H. Yoder (HP, 1989), 394 (adapted). Based on Luke 15:21; 19:1-10

# 260 Prayer

Lord Jesus,
    take from us all obstacles
    that take room from you in our hearts.
Forgive our sins, heal our diseases.
Restore to us the joy of our salvation.
Give those we have sinned against,
    grace to forgive us
and give us grace
    to forgive those who have sinned against us.
Make this holy Supper
    a foretaste of eternal life with you. Amen.

—John D. Rempel, New York City

# 261 Lord's Supper

Lord of hosts, preparer of this table;
    prepare us.
The feast is ready. Make *us* ready.
We hear the promises of Scripture:
    to lift the veil of self-righteousness,
    to destroy the covering of gloom,
    to shatter the barriers of ignorance.

Enable us to come to this banquet rejoicing,
> knowing we are clothed in forgiveness and mercy
> and gifted with the joy of salvation. Amen.

—Judith G. Kipp, in *For All Who Minister* (copyright © 1993, Brethren Press, Elgin, Ill.; used by permission)

# 262 Prayer

Merciful God,
> we do not come to this table because we are good.
We come because we are sinful and need forgiveness
> and because Jesus welcomed sinners.
We come because we are hungry for life and need to be fed.
Merciful God, forgive us and feed us.

We come in gratitude and wonder,
> to offer ourselves in worship.
Receive us and our praise
> through Jesus Christ our Lord. Amen.

—Phil Bedsworth, Hesston, Kan., in his notebooks

# 263 A Prayer at Communion

O Lord, almighty God, we are assembled to commemorate
> the broken body and shed blood
> of your dear Son, Jesus Christ.
Prepare our hearts for this ceremony;
make us worthy as spiritual pilgrims
> to partake of these holy emblems.
Help us to understand the mystery of this sign,
> that we may observe it to your honor
> and the welfare of our souls.

We freely confess all our sins,
    our weaknesses and shortcomings,
and come to you without defense,
    with no righteousness of our own.
We seek only the righteousness of Christ
    which he obtained for us
    through his bitter death on the cross.

May our hungry souls receive nourishment
    through the grace and gift of your Holy Spirit
    to partake of the emblems of Christ's body and blood.
May Christ abide in us and we in him
    that his suffering be not in vain.

We thank you from the depth of our hearts
    for the consolation and help you give us.
Keep us the remaining years of our lives
    in faith, in love and patience,
    and help us willingly to carry the cross you give us.
Let us serve you the whole of our lives
    in temperance, righteousness, and a godly fear,
    growing in grace and virtue,
    to the honor of your holy name.
Our Father who art in heaven. . . .

—*Die ernsthafte Christenpflicht* (original, 1739; HP, 1991), 120-121; trans. in *A Devoted Christian's Prayer Book* (Aylmer, Ont.: Pathway, 1984), 45-46 (adapted)

# 264 Prayer

Gracious God,
    pour out your Holy Spirit upon us
    and upon these your gifts of bread and cup.
In broken bread and shared cup,
    make us the body of Christ
    and confirm your covenant with us.

By your Spirit bind us to the living Christ,
>that we may be bound in faith to all who share the feast,
>united in service throughout the world.

Give us strength to serve you faithfully
>until the promised day of resurrection,
>when with all the redeemed,
>we feast with you in your kingdom.

Through Christ, with Christ, in Christ,
>in the unity of the Holy Spirit,
>all glory and honor are yours, God of all ages,
>now and forever. Amen.

—*Liturgical Year,* Supplemental Liturgical Resource 7 (Louisville:
Westminster/John Knox, © 1992; used by permission of Westminster John
Knox Press), 148 (adapted)

# 265 Prayer

O God of unity and completeness,
>your image lies within our hearts;
>your Spirit calls us to each other.

We are your children, and we seek your blessing;
>together we lift our hearts to your all-embracing love.
>together we trust in your all-encompassing kindness.

Heal our divisions, give us unity,
>deliver us from prejudice, give us great charity.

As we receive these symbols of life and death,
>let us declare our peace with you
>and with each other,
>through Jesus Christ, your Son,
>>who taught us to pray, "Our Father . . ." *(Lord's Prayer)*

—Arlene M. Mark

## 266 Worldwide Communion Sunday Responsive Reading

L: Let us bow down in worship;
    let us kneel before the Lord our Maker,

**P: the one God and Father of all,**
    **who is above all, and through all, and in us all.**

L: We are children of God
    through faith in Christ Jesus,

**P: so there is neither Jew nor Greek, slave nor free,**
    **male nor female, for we are all one in Jesus Christ.**
    **Therefore, let us keep the feast.**

L: Is not the bread that we break
    a participation in the body of Christ?

**P: Is not the cup of thanksgiving**
    **a participation in the blood of Christ?**

*All: Because there is one loaf,*
    *we who are many, are one body;*
    *for we all partake of the one loaf.*
    *In Christ, we who are many form one body,*
    *and each member belongs to all the others.*
    *Therefore, let us make every effort*
    *to keep the unity of the Spirit*
    *through the bond of peace.*

—Arlene M. Mark. MPH Bulletin, 10-3-82. Based on Ps. 95:6; Eph. 4:6; Col. 3:11;
1 Cor. 10:16-17; Eph. 4:3

## 267 Responsive Reading for Communion Service

L: At this common meeting place of the Lord's table,
    we enter into a spirit of togetherness,
    becoming one body in Christ,
    all members one of another.

**P: We are all followers of Christ**
**and share the bread and cup as an act of unity,**
**recognizing our joining with all believers**
**everywhere in all times.**
L: We remember the price paid for our redemption
so that we may have life in abundance.
**P: We remember the presence of the risen Christ among us**
**and recommit ourselves to the way of the cross.**
L: Let us make ready our hearts and minds,
leaving judgment of others aside,
considering only our own relationship to God.
**P: We come as penitent believers, asking forgiveness,**
**accepting God's transforming grace**
**and recommitting our lives totally to Christ as Lord.**
L: Let us keep the feast;
for the spiritual food is the gift of Christ to us.
**P: Let us experience the mystery,**
**for here Christ gives himself to us again,**
**and we are renewed on our spiritual journey,**
**looking forward to the feast of the redeemed**
**in the age to come.**

—Arlene M. Mark

# Ministries

## Wedding

### 268 Congregational Response

_____ and _____,
we join with you in the sacredness of this hour.
We honor your vows
    to be loyal and loving to each other
    so long as you both shall live.
We give our pledge,
    as family, friends, and faith community,
    to support and encourage you in fulfilling your covenant.
We commend you to God,
    who has promised to strengthen you,
    help you, and uphold you.
Have faith in God's power
    which brought you together and can keep you together.
And may the grace and peace of our Lord Jesus Christ
    fill your days so that you may live together
    in joyous harmony. Amen.

—Arlene M. Mark

# 269 Wedding Prayer

Eternal God,
> creator and preserver of all life,
> author of salvation, giver of all grace:
> bless and sanctify with your Holy Spirit
> _____ and _____, who come now
> asking for your blessing upon their marriage.

Grant that they may give their vows to each other
> in the strength of your steadfast love.

Enable them to grow in love and peace
> with you and with each other all their days.

Because of the love they know,
> may they reach out in concern and service to the world,
> through Jesus Christ our Lord. Amen.

—From *A Service for the Recognition or the Blessing of a Civil Marriage and an Order for the Reaffirmation of the Marriage Covenant* (© 1979 by Abingdon; © 1992 UMPH; used by permission; adapted)

# Funeral

# 270 Scriptures of Promise and Hope

L: O magnify the Lord with me;
> let us exalt God's name together.
> Cast your burden on the Lord,
> and he will sustain you.

**P: Our help is in the name of the Lord,**
> **who made heaven and earth.**

L: Blessed are those who die in the Lord.
> They will rest from their labor,
> and their deeds will follow them.

**P: None of us lives alone,**
> **and none of us dies alone.**
> **If we live, we live to the Lord;**
> **if we die, we die to the Lord.**

L: Nothing will be able to separate us
from the love of God in Christ Jesus our Lord.
**P: I know that my Redeemer lives,
and that at the last he will stand upon the earth.**
L: When this perishable body puts on imperishability,
and this mortal body puts on immortality,
then the saying that is written will be fulfilled:
*All: "Death has been swallowed up in victory."*
*"Where, O death, is your victory?*
*Where, O death, is your sting?"*
*But thanks be to God,*
*who gives us the victory through our Lord Jesus Christ.*

—Arlene M. Mark. Based on Pss. 34:3; 55:22; 124:8; Rev. 14:13; Rom. 14:7-8;
8:38-39; Job 19:25; 1 Cor. 15:54-57

# 271  Funeral Call to Worship

Love the Lord, all you saints.
The Lord preserves the faithful.
Be strong, and let your heart take courage,
all you who wait for the Lord.

We have gathered here today to praise God
and to celebrate the memory of _____,
a beloved *son/daughter/(relationship term)*.
Together we grieve in our loss;
together we find comfort and strength.
Together we struggle with the pain of death;
together we rejoice in God's eternal resurrection.
For we know that the souls of the righteous
are in the hands of God,
that God is our refuge and strength,
a very present help in trouble.
Therefore we will not fear.

For in God's presence there is fullness of joy;
>    in God's right hand are pleasures forevermore.

—Arlene M. Mark. Based on Deut. 6:5; Ps. 31:24; Wisd. 3:1; Pss. 46:1-2; 16:11

# 272 Funeral Prayer

Almighty God,
you have been our dwelling place
>    throughout all generations;
>    you are our guardian in life and death.
By you we were brought into being,
>    and in your care and keeping we leave this life.
Through the resurrection of Christ Jesus,
>    we will live eternally with you and all the saints.

We praise you for all your servants,
>    who, having lived in faith and discipleship,
>    are now at rest with you.

Our joy is to commit our loved one, _____,
>    into the never-ending majesty of your presence,
>    where *he/she* can forever give you ceaseless praise.
We thank you that for *him/her* the pain
>    of life and death is past.
*He/she* has fought the good fight,
>    finished the course, and kept the faith.
Now *he/she* claims the crown of righteousness
>    which the Lord has reserved for this servant.

God of hope,
>    fill us who grieve with peace and assurance
>    that we will one day stand with _____
>    and all your disciples who have labored for you.

Together we will surround your throne
in your glorious kingdom
prepared for those who love and serve you.
Through Christ the resurrected one, we pray. Amen.

—Arlene M. Mark. Based on Ps. 90:1; 2 Tim. 4:7-8; Rev. 22:1-5

# 273  Funeral Prayer

Eternal God,
in you we live and move and have our being.
You are never far from us, but you are most near
when we deeply feel our need for you.
Reveal yourself to us in this hour
as the God who watches over all our ways
and turns even death and sorrow into blessing
for those who love you.
In sadness of heart we have gathered for these last
solemn and tender moments of faith and love.
Take from us the shadows that surround us,
and give us your light to see the whole of life.
Help us to know that you are the God of the living:
with you there are no dead;
our departed loved one is at home with you forevermore.
Help us to confirm that death, instead of ending life,
is the beginning of larger and more abundant life.

Comfort the hearts heavy with sorrow;
befriend us in loneliness.
Grant us faith to look beyond this scene of mourning
to your heavenly kingdom,
where earth's tears are dried,
earth's broken friendship is restored, and

earth's unfinished task of glorifying you can last forever;
through Jesus Christ our Lord. Amen.

# 274  Prayer

Eternal God,
　　who changes not in life or death,
be our assurance as we mourn our loved one
　　and commit *him/her* to your care.
Give us relief from grief and anger;
　　　open our hearts to your never-failing love.

Holy Spirit,
　　who guides through all of life,
be our peace in the mystery of death.
Give us your comforting presence,
　　so that death will not be defeat,
　　but a meeting with the God we love.

Jesus Christ,
　　who passed from death to life,
be our triumph over suffering and death.
Give us sustaining grace and assurance,
　　as we await your coming again
　　to receive us unto yourself. Amen.

—Arlene M. Mark

# 275 Prayer

We give back to you, O God,
    those whom you gave to us.
You did not lose them
    when you gave them to us,
    and we do not lose them by their return to you.
Your dear Son has taught us
    that life eternal and love cannot die.
Death is only a horizon,
    and a horizon is only the limit of our sight.
Open our eyes to see more clearly,
    and draw us closer to you,
    that we may know we are nearer to our loved ones
    who are with you.
You have told us that you are preparing a place for us;
    prepare us also for that happy place,
    that where you are we may also be always,
    O dear Lord of life and death. Amen.

—William Penn (1644-1718), in *The Oxford Book of Prayer*, ed. by George
Appleton (New York: Oxford Univ. Press, 1985), no. 541

# Child Blessing

# 276 Ceremony of Child Dedication

*Parents are invited to bring their children to the front as the congrega-*
*tion sings "Children of the Heavenly Father." Others significant to each*
*child may stand behind the parents to form a "cloud of witnesses."*

L: Parents, you may name the child you present
    before the congregation.
*(Parents introduce the children.)*

L: We praise God for each child presented here today.
　　We bless God that in his fatherly goodness,
　　　　he sent Jesus Christ, our Lord and Savior,
　　　　who gave mercy to the innocent children,
　　　　and took them in his arms,
　　　　and assured them of the kingdom of God.

**People: We thank God for these precious children.**

L: Dear parents, you are surrounded by these witnesses
　　　　who are supporting you in your parental task.
　　In this public act of dedication, you are presenting
　　　　yourselves and your *child/children* to the Lord.
　　You are coming with a prayer that God may give you grace
　　　　to fulfill your parental role.

**Parents:** *(praying)* **Our heavenly Father,**
　　　　**we thank you for our child.**
　　　　**We accept this child as a sacred trust.**
　　　　**Give us divine resources**
　　　　**to nurture, to love, to counsel,**
　　　　**to teach, to train, to show.**
　　　　**Give us your Spirit with strength and wisdom.**
　　　　**May our child one day receive Jesus as Savior and Lord.**
　　　　**We surrender our child to you,**
　　　　**to be kept by your power,**
　　　　**to be used in your service,**
　　　　**and finally, to be received into your presence.**
　　　　**Through Jesus Christ, our Lord. Amen.**


*(Congregational Response)*

We give thanks for your statement of dedication,
　　and we promise, with God's help,
　　to support you in the task of parenting.
As others have encouraged us in our faith journey,
　　we will stand with you to witness to your child
　　about the Christian way.

In concern for this little one,
    we will carefully model
    Christian faith in our actions and words.
May this child know abundant love
    and follow the path to life eternal.

—First ten lines based on Pilgram Marpeck (1532), in *The Writings of P. M.*
(Classics of the Radical Reformation, 2), trans. and ed. by Wm. Klassen and
Walter Klaassen (HP, 1978), 147; and Mark 10:13-16; the next part by Russell
Krabill, Elkhart, Ind., in MPH Bulletin, 8-20-89; and the congregational
response by Arlene M. Mark

# 277 Prayer at Infant Dedication

God of us all,
you tend us like a kindly shepherd
    and carry the lambs in your arms.
Keep this little one in your loving care.
In infancy, may _____ be loved
    by parents and friends who know your grace and joy.
As a child, may _____ absorb from living models
    all that is good and true and pure and of good report
    so that *he/she* may happily learn the Christian way.
When a youth, may _____ be guided
    by precept, example, and invitation
    to choose Jesus Christ as *his/her* Savior and Lord.
As a member of your flock, may _____ fulfill
    the high hopes of all who share in this blessing today.
Shepherd _____ through life,
    call _____ by name,
    and lead *him/her* by refreshing streams.
And if there are valleys of dark shadows,
    be the source of strength and courage,
    through Jesus Christ our Lord. Amen.

—Arlene M. Mark. Based on Ps. 23; Isa. 40:11; Phil. 4:8-9

# 278  A Prayer of Parents for Their Children

Dear God and Father, Creator and Guardian of all living beings,
give us the grace to bring up our children
    in the discipline and instruction of the Lord.
Help us to be an example of all virtue.
Give our children grace and the gifts of the Spirit
    so they will profit from the counsel we give them.
Fill them with desire to do your will
    and claim your promises.

Favor them with true knowledge,
    and keep them from all idolatry and false teachings.
Give them a faithful and obedient mind,
    with true wisdom and understanding.
Let them increase in wisdom and stature,
    and in divine and human favor.

Implant in their hearts a fervent love for your holy Word.
    May they be attentive to prayer and devotions.
Protect them from the evil influences of this world,
    so they will not be led astray by evil companions.

Be a shield to them in all kinds of danger
    lest they be overtaken by a violent or untimely death.

Let your church here on earth be preserved and enlarged
    by us, our children, descendants, and all whom you call.
Finally, may we all meet in your eternal heavenly kingdom,
    to sing the new song of joy and praise to you forever.

This we pray in Jesus' name. Amen.

—*Die ernsthafte Christenpflicht* (original, 1739; HP, 1991), 144-145; trans. in *A Devoted Christian's Prayer Book* (Aylmer, Ont.: Pathway, 1984), 35-37 (adapted). Based on Eph. 6:4; Luke 2:52

# 279 A Blessing for Children

1: Children
   are God's most sacred surprise,
   a light in the eyes,
   a lift to the heart,
   a storyline's continuation.

*All:* ***Thank you, God, for children;***
   ***bless them, everyone.***

2: Children
   mirror mystery.
   Children
   are God's preferred way of being,
   preferred way of seeing
   the world and all its people.

*All:* ***Teach us God, through children;***
   ***bless them, everyone.***

1: Our children
   are not our children.
   They are given to us
   and pass through us
   into worlds of their own making,
   into risks of their own taking,
   into futures we will not know.

*All:* ***Help us, God, to let our children go;***
   ***bless them, everyone.***

2: When children feel
   they are included,
   a little hope gleams on all horizons,
   a new dream dances in our generation,
   and seeds are sown for a new creation.

*All:* ***Help us, God, to grow through our children;***
   ***bless them, everyone.***

> *All:*   *All of us are children:*
> *children of God,*
> *children of children,*
> *children whose children*
> *are children of children.*
> *Let us be reconciled*
> *to the child within,*
> *so that love can live on*
> *beyond us*
> *forever.*
> *We praise you, God, and we thank you*
> *in the name of our children.*
> *Bless them, everyone.*

—Miriam T. Winter, *WomanWisdom* (New York: Crossroad, 1991), 111-112 (adapted)

# 280  A Blessing for Children

Save me, O Lord, from selfishness—
    especially when I am saying my prayers.
When I ask something for myself,
    may I remember all the others
    who want it as well,
    and never let me forget the boys and girls
    of other lands as well as at home
    who are hungry and lonely and unhappy.
So I pray now:
    God bless all children everywhere.

—Donald O. Soper, *Children's Prayer Time* (Epworth Press)

# 281 A Service to Celebrate a Youth's Growing Faith

L: *(to all)* Today is a very important day for _____.
   As a congregation we are celebrating a passage
      into a new phase of life for *him/her.*
   _____ has made a decision
      to invite Jesus Christ into *his/her* life.

L: *(to youth)* _____, we have watched you grow
      through the years.
   We respect the ways you have been growing
      physically, emotionally, and spiritually.
   We are excited by the change you want to make in your life.
   You are making a statement that you are aware
      of Christ's love for you and your love for Christ.
   We recognize this event in your journey of faith
      and encourage you to continue to grow
      in your commitment to Christ.
   We invite you to read your chosen Scripture
      and to share your statement of faith.

*(Youth reads a Scripture and may share about the experience leading to this commitment. Leader may invite those relating to the youth to form a circle of love and support around* him/her *for the blessing.)*

P: **You are a special part of this congregation.**
      **There is no one else in the whole world quite like you.**
      **We are proud of you and we love you.**
   **We recognize your commitment to Christ.**
      **We accept with seriousness your statement of dedication**
      **and intent to grow**
      **in the grace and knowledge of our Lord Jesus Christ.**
   **We bless you to grow, in body and mind and spirit,**
      **in surprising ways.**
      **We bless you to explore life, to be adventurous**
      **in discovering who God has created you to be.**

   **We bless you to make mistakes, and to learn from them,**
      **even if the consequences are difficult and painful.**

**We bless you to succeed in life, to be a productive,
healthy, and happy member of God's family.
We will support you with our love, counsel, and prayers,
and walk with you on your journey of faith.**

L: *(prayer)* O God,
we thank you for _____'s acknowledgment
of your importance in *his/her* life.
It is good when one affirms faith in you,
for it renews us all.
Help us to be responsible in furthering
_____'s journey of faith.
May we be examples and teachers
in the days and years to come.
Grant that _____ may continue to grow
into full commitment of *his/her* life
to Jesus Christ and the church. Amen.

—Adapted from "A Service to Celebrate a Youth's Growing Faith," in *For All Who Minister* (copyright © 1993, Brethren Press, Elgin, Ill.; used by permission)

# Reception of New Members

## 282 Congregational Response to New Members

The church is a body of believers,
joined together on earth to proclaim the love of God
and to follow Christ's example of life and ministry.
We welcome you into our congregation.
You expect us to provide
scriptural nourishment for your growth,
support in your joys and sorrows,
and spiritual discernment in decision making.
We accept your expectations
and pray God's strength and wisdom to meet your needs.

We expect you to share *yourself/yourselves* with us
 in calling us to faithfulness,
 and contributing your abilities and gifts
 for the common good of the body of Christ.
We accept your commitment to Christ and this body
 and welcome you warmly in this covenant making
 to be God's people together.
Be the church with us,
 assemble with us as a community of disciples,
 strengthen our separation from the world to God,
 and be alert to the power of the Spirit.
We are blessed that you have chosen us
 to be your spiritual family.
 Let joy and praise unite our hearts,
 and may our joining together
 mutually bless and strengthen us
 as we follow Christ together.

—Arlene M. Mark

# Congregational Commitment

*Since our life in the congregation continues year after year, there should be times to renew our membership covenant.*

## 283 Recommitment Covenant

We commit ourselves to follow Jesus Christ,
 through whom God has reconciled the world,
 and in whom we continue the work of reconciliation.
We commit ourselves to each other and this congregation,
 promising to love our brothers and sisters in God's family.
We will share our time, our decisions, our love,
 our talents and possessions for everyone's good.

We commit ourselves to care for the world,
> to bring good news to the poor,
> to set free the oppressed,
> and to proclaim Jesus as liberator and Lord.

We commit ourselves to the way of the cross,
> to a life of simplicity and prayer.

In this we will find our joy, our peace, and our life.

—Grace Mennonite Church, St. Catharines, Ont., Bulletin, 12-31-78, in *Baptism and Church Membership* (Worship Series, 3), ed. by James Waltner (MPH, 1979), 44-45 (adapted)

# 284 Responsive Reading

L: Covenant with me
> to spread community
> to worlds beyond this place.

**P: Sing anew God's praise,**
> **accept our ministry,**
> **begin the healing task.**

L: See afresh again
> God's image in each one;
> reflect that face ourselves.

**P: Unite with those who love**
> **enough to move toward change,**
> **empowered by the Spirit.**

*All: Go on our way in joy;*
> *create a celebration.*
> *God's likeness lives in us.*

—*Women's Prayer Services*, ed. by Iben Gjerding and Katherine Kinnamon (Mystic, Conn.: Twenty-Third Publications, 1983), 46

# 285 Statement of Covenant

We are not called to be fearful,
    we are called to love.
We are not called to be perfect,
    we are called to be faithful.
We are not called to be fearless,
    we are called to be obedient.
We are not called to be all-knowing,
    we are called to believe.
We are not called to claim,
    we are called to give.
We are not called to be victorious,
    we are called to be courageous.
We are not called to lord it over others,
    we are called to serve.

For it is in serving that we shall reign,
    it is through courage that we shall find victory,
    it is in giving all that we shall gain all,
    it is in believing that we shall find certainty,
    it is in obedience that we shall overcome,
    it is in faithfulness that we shall find perfection,
    it is in loving that we shall dispel fear,
    it is in slavery to Christ and his justice
        that we shall find freedom, now and forever,
        for ourselves and for the world. Amen.

—Allan Boesak, "Address to the General Council," in *Seoul 1989: Proceedings of the 22nd General Council,* ed. by Edmond Perret (World Council of Reformed Churches, 1990, © World Alliance of Reformed Churches), 154 (adapted)

## 286 Statement of Church Covenant

We covenant together, God helping us:
   to love the Lord with all our hearts,
   to keep our lives pure and yielded to God,
   to fellowship with God in personal and family devotions,
   to give gladly of our time, talents, and possessions,
   to be faithful in meeting together and in Christian service.
We covenant together, God helping us:
   to love each other as ourselves,
   to serve each other in humble and sacrificial love,
   to admonish, encourage, and forgive one another,
   to be accountable to each other,
   to submit to the loving discipline of our community of faith,
   to bear one another's burdens.
We covenant together, God helping us:
   to live out discipleship, guided by our Christian community,
   to be separated from the world's evil by transformed minds,
   to seek peace and pursue it in our daily living,
   to trust in God's love as our protection,
   to proclaim the good news of salvation
      through our words and consistent testimony,
   to look forward with joyful anticipation
      to the gathering in of the saints
      when Christ will return to judge the living and the dead
      and there will be a new heaven and new earth.

—*Worship Hymnal* (Fresno, Calif.: General Conference of Mennonite Brethren
Churches, 1971), 774 (adapted)

# Commissioning

## 287 Commissioning

L: Through the Spirit, God gives many gifts,
   all of them useful in building the church.

God calls all of us to the ministry of reconciliation.
Each of us thus shares in the servanthood of all.

L: *(to assignees)* As you accept your service assignments,
   your tasks become our tasks,
   your covenant becomes our covenant.
We therefore join in this commissioning charge.

P: **We commission you in the name of our Lord Jesus Christ.**
   **As you go, proclaim the good news,**
      **"The kingdom of God has come near."**
   **Call people to faith in Christ.**
      **Care for the sick in body and soul.**
   **Be messengers of the healing and victory over evil**
      **that comes with God's powerful reign.**

Assignees: With joy, we accept this charge
      and count ourselves as ambassadors for Christ,
      bearing the message of reconciliation, forgiveness,
      and a new creation in Christ.

P: **As God's Spirit calls and the church commissions,**
      **the servants of Christ are scattered in places of need.**
   **We accept your service as an extension of this congregation**
      **and pledge our support to make your ministry effective.**
   **We join you in affirming the priority of Christ's kingdom.**
   **May God protect and strengthen you in all circumstances,**
      **and grant you a deep love for those whom you serve.**
   **We will keep praying for you,**
      **that Christ may be seen through you in word and deed.**

—John H. Mosemann (1967), in *The Mennonite Hymnal* (HP, 1969), 732 (adapted). Based on 1 Cor. 12—14; Matt. 10:5-8; Luke 9:2; 2 Cor. 5:18-20

## 288  Installation of Church Leaders

P: *(to appointees)* **Dear friends, you have been called by God**
      **and chosen by the people of God**
      **for leadership in this church.**
   **This ministry is a blessing and a serious responsibility.**

> **Led by the Spirit, we recognize your special gifts**
> > **and call you to work among us and for us.**
> **In love we thank you for accepting your obligation,**
> **and we challenge you to offer your best**
> > **to the Lord, to this people,**
> > **and to our ministry in the world.**
> **We bid you to live a life in Christ**
> > **and make him known in your witness and your work.**

L/P: *(prayer)* Almighty God,
> pour out your blessings upon this your servant
> > who have been given particular ministries in your church.
> Grant them grace to give themselves
> > wholeheartedly in your service.
> Keep before them the example of our Lord,
> > who did not think first of himself,
> > but gave himself for us all.
> Let them share his ministry and consecration,
> > that they may enter into his joy.
> Guide them in their work.
> Reward their faithfulness with the knowledge
> > that through them your purposes are accomplished;
> > through Jesus Christ our Lord. Amen.

L: *(to congregation)* Dear friends,
> rejoice that God provides laborers for the vineyards.
> Will you do all you can to assist and encourage them
> > in the responsibilities to which they have been called?
> Will you give them your cooperation,
> > your counsel, and your prayers?

**P: We will.**

—From *An Order for the Installation or Recognition of Leaders in the Church and an Order for the Installation of Church School Workers* (© 1964, 1965 by Board of Publication of the Methodist Church, Inc.; © 1984 by Abingdon Press; © 1992 UMPH; renewal © 1992 UMPH; used by permission)

# 289 Prayer of Commitment

L: Blessed are you, O God,
  who graces each of us
  with skills, talents, abilities, and opportunities.

P: **To you, and to our sisters and brothers,
  we offer these gifts.**

L: We pledge to live no more unto ourselves
  but to love and serve your purposes.

P: **We commit ourselves, O God,
  for service and ministry,
  in our congregation, community, and throughout the
    world.**

L: Let your wisdom teach us
  and your power enable us.

P: **Unite us with all Christians
  as we celebrate your reign,
  for the common good of all your people. Amen.**

—Keith Graber Miller, Goshen, Ind., in MPH Bulletin, 1-19-92 (adapted)

# 290 Litany of Dedication

L: Almighty God,
  we gather today to dedicate ourselves anew
    to your love that is ever seeking fullness in our hearts.
  We thank you that we are called
    into the fellowship and service of Jesus Christ,
  and that Christ is able and willing to use us
    to proclaim the kingdom of his love.

P: **We dedicate our gifts of speech, conversation, and writing
  to the cause of peace, love, and reconciliation.**

L: We thank you that we are called to use
  the work of our hands,
    the opportunities of professional and business life,
    and the occasions of conversation and fellowship—

to share with others the love of Christ.

**P:  We dedicate our gifts of skill, integrity, and craftsmanship
    to the cause of friendship and Christian witness.**

L:  We thank you that we are called
    into the church of Jesus Christ
    to extend his healing reign,
    to keep alive the conscience of the world,
    and to carry out the great commission.

**P:  We dedicate our gifts of leadership, teaching, and friendship
    to the cause of true community and conscience building.**

L:  We thank you that we are called into conversation
    with those of other faiths, other nationalities,
    in the spirit of Christ, who calls all to follow him.

**P:  We dedicate our denominational insights and treasures
    to the one church,
    and we seek to learn from all
    who profess faith in Christ.**

L:  We thank you that we are called to share with all humanity,
    regardless of creed, class, or color,
    what we have gained from Christ.

**P:  We dedicate to the human family
    our gifts of persuasion, conviction, and experience,
    seeking the good of all
    and the triumph of the kingdom of God. Amen.**

—W. B. J. Martin, *Acts of Worship* (Nashville: Abingdon, 1960), 178-179
(adapted)

# 291  Prayer for Faithful Workers

O Lord of the harvest,
    truly the harvest is great
    but the laborers are few.
    Awaken among us, O Lord,
    faithful teachers, fervent workers,
    who will plant the seeds of truth

throughout the world.
Give us those who are godly minded,
 have found grace in your eyes,
 and are able to work according to your will.
May they preach your word
 in the power of the Spirit,
 in meekness and sincerity,
 to the honor and glory of your name.
We pray that your ministry may be continued
 through the laying on of holy hands,
 and be directed to our great spiritual needs,
 to your honor and glory
 and for the welfare of our souls and bodies,
 in time and eternity.
In Jesus' name. Amen.

—*Die ernsthafte Christenpflicht* (original, 1739; HP, 1991), 43-44; *A Devoted Christian's Prayer Book* (Aylmer, Ont.: Pathway, 1984), 23-24 (adapted). Based on Matt. 9:35-38

# 292 Prayer of Dedication

Holiest of all,
you call us to witness your divine splendor;
 you touch our lips, and with our voices we praise you.
You are uplifted, yet you stoop to hear us,
 cleansing our guilt and forgiving our sin.
We are here in response to your calling;
 we offer our gifts of time, talents, and tithe.
Send us forth as your witnesses,
 so that hosts may know you
 and give you glory. Amen.

—James G. Kirk, *When We Gather· Year C* (Philadelphia: Geneva, 1985; used by permission of Westminster John Knox Press), 41

## 293 Prayer

Come, O Holy Spirit, O Sanctifying Spirit,
  fill our hearts,
  fill our lives
  with the feel of your fiery presence,
  so that all we do,
  all that we are,
  comes from you within us.
Anoint us now,
  so that from this day
  we are your disciples only,
  committed to carrying out faithfully
  your mission in the world,
  now and always. Amen.

—Miriam T. Winter, *WomanWisdom* (New York: Crossroad, 1991), 68

## 294 Litany of Commissioning Sunday School Teachers

L: O God, you have gifted the persons
  who are committed to teach this year.
  Fill them with the love of Christ and the power of the Spirit
  as they carry out this ministry.
*Teachers: Grant us wisdom, patience, and hope when we falter.*
  *Give us joy in our task.*
  *Keep us faithful to our commitment to teach.*
**Classes: Help us, through prayer and words of encouragement,**
  **freely to support those who teach.**
  **Give us grace to forgive when necessary**
  **and presence of mind to reassure teachers along the way.**

***All: Let this new Sunday school year
be a blessing to our congregation,
a time for spiritual enrichment and growth.
In Jesus' name. Amen.***

—Sunnyside Mennonite Church, Elkhart, Ind., Bulletin, 9-12-93 (adapted;
source unknown)

# Reconciliation

## 295 Statement on Reconciliation

*(in unison)*
As Christ's reconciling community,
    let us show compassion and mercy.
Let us reflect God's boundless grace
    and deal tenderly with any one who has sinned.
Let us make every effort to keep the unity of the Spirit
    through the bond of peace.
Let us be a place of pardon
    and a haven of hope for those in despair.
Let us live together in faithful obedience,
    supported and secure in our oneness,
    companions in conformity to Christ,
    to whom be glory in the church
    throughout all generations, forever and ever. Amen.

—Arlene M. Mark. Based on Eph. 4:3; 3:21

## 296 Prayer of Reconciliation

Holy God, we thank you that you deal with us
    not according to our sins
    nor punish us as we deserve,
but receive us according to your overflowing grace
    and your unmeasurable mercy.

You receive us as we are;
    you show us what we can be.
You have come to us in Jesus Christ to share our common lot
    and to reconcile us to yourself.
Sweep over us with your Spirit,
    change us by your love,
    resolve our alienation.
Let us be made whole to sing with joy before you
    and live to your glory in the world.

—United Church of Christ Statement of Faith, in *Touch Holiness*, ed. by Ruth C.
Duck and Maren C. Tirrabassi (Cleveland: Pilgrim Press, 1990), 105 (adapted)

# 297  Ministry of Reconciliation

L: Since we are justified by faith,
    we have peace with God
    through our Lord Jesus Christ.

P: **God proves his love for us**
    **in that while we were still sinners**
    **Christ died for us.**

L: While we were enemies,
    we were reconciled to God
    through the death of his Son.
    Much more surely will we be saved by his life.

P: **For in Jesus all the fullness of God**
    **was pleased to dwell,**
    **and through him, God was pleased**
    **to reconcile to himself all things.**

L: For Christ is our peace;
    in his flesh he has broken down
    the dividing wall between us,
    that he might create in himself one new humanity.

P:  **All this is from God,**
   **who reconciled us to himself through Christ,**
   **and has given us the ministry of reconciliation.**
*All:  So we are ambassadors for Christ!*

—Susan Mark Landis, Orrville, Ohio, in MBCM materials (adapted). Based on
2 Cor. 5; Eph. 2; Col. 1

# 298  Prayer of Healing and Reconciliation

Creator God,
belonging to you,
  we confess our responsibility
  for the brokenness of this earth
  and the people of this earth.
We are part of the community of the covenant,
  seeking forgiveness for indifference.
We accept the challenge
  of beginning anew in your strength and love.
Creator God,
we give thanks for the mountains, the seas,
  the valleys, and the trees;
  all part of your creation.
We give thanks for the covenant of a people
  who understand your liberation to include the earth,
  which cries out against our thoughtlessness.
Creator God,
may we be guided to deeper understanding
  of the covenant with creation.
May we care for all of life,
  as the elders have taught.
May we honor those who dare to dream
  of recreated global harmony.

—Urbane Peachey, in Akron (Pa.) Mennonite Church Bulletin, 7-5-92

# 299 Prayer of Reconciliation

L: Let us pray to the Lord.

P: **Almighty God,**
   **we confess that you have broken the tyranny of sin**
   **and given us glorious liberty as children of God.**

L: For God was pleased to have
   all his fullness dwell in Christ,
   and through Christ to reconcile all things to God,
   whether things on earth or things in heaven,
   by making peace through Christ's blood shed on the cross.

P: **Thank you, O Lord, for coming to us**
   **and restoring us to full fellowship with you.**

L: If anyone is in Christ, there is a new creation;
   the old has gone, the new has come!

P: **We are grateful, O Christ,**
   **that you have transformed our inner natures**
   **and renewed us for your service.**

L: All this is from God,
   who reconciled us to himself through Christ,
   and has given to us the ministry of reconciliation.

P: **Because we now are God's friends instead of enemies,**
   **we have become partners with God**
   **in sharing the gift of peace with others.**

L: We therefore are Christ's ambassadors,
   as though God were making the appeal through us.
   I implore you on Christ's behalf: be reconciled to God!

P: **We accept this call, and in the power of the Holy Spirit,**
   **we pledge ourselves to proclaim**
   **God's good news of reconciliation. Amen.**

—Dan Schrock, Columbus, Ohio (adapted). Based on Col. 1:19-20; 2 Cor. 5:17-20

# Anointing

## 300 Prayer

Loving God,
Lord of all health and wholeness,
    you are source of our life
    and fulfillment of our death.

We come to you now with varied needs.
    Into your gentle care we place ourselves
    and our loved ones who are ill.

Be for us now
    light to brighten our darkness,
    strength to transform our weakness,
    and comfort in the midst of our pain.

We ask this in the power of the Spirit
    through Christ, our Lord. Amen.

—Mary F. Duffy, *Anointing of the Sick (Alternative Futures for Worship*, 7), ed. by Peter E. Fink (Collegeville: Liturgical Press, 1987), 117-118

## 301 Prayer

Almighty God,
we pray that *(name, names)*
    may be comforted in their suffering and made whole.
When they are afraid, give them courage;
when they feel weak, grant them strength;
when they are afflicted, afford them patience;
when they are lost, offer them hope;
when they are alone, move us to their side;
when death comes, open your arms to receive *him/her/them.*
In the name of Jesus Christ we pray. Amen.

—From *The United Methodist Book of Worship,* (copyright © 1992 by UMPH; used by permission)

## Congregational Meeting

# 302 Prayer for Business Meeting

Our Lord,
we thank you that in our work and worship
    we are assembled in your name,
your Son has been among us,
    and your Holy Spirit has guided us.

As we meet together in this business session,
be our center:
    in our uncertainties, give us direction;
    in our differences, give us understanding;
    in our reporting, give us honesty;
    in our planning, give us boldness;
    in our deciding, give us deference.

Never let us forget that we are your servants,
    called to proclaim the reign of God,
    committed to follow Christ in life,
    united as one body in Christ.

We are not sufficient of ourselves;
    provide our sufficiency.
We are not wise of ourselves;
    provide our wisdom.
We are not confident of ourselves;
    provide our confidence
that we may be faithful in your service
    and abounding in hope
for the sake of your kingdom. Amen.

—Arlene M. Mark

# Table Graces

## 303 Prayer for Food

O God,
as we come together
for the food your love has given us,
we remember Christ was made known to his disciples
in the breaking of bread.
May he be with us,
and may his Spirit
enter into all we say and do. Amen.

—Adapted from *Lift Up Your Hearts* by Walter Russell Bowie (copyright renewal © 1984 by Mrs. Jean B. Evans, Mrs. Elizabeth Chapman, and Mrs. Walter Russell Bowie, Jr.; used by permission of the publisher, Abingdon Press)

## 304 Table Grace

O gracious God,
when you open your hand,
you satisfy the desires of every living thing.
Bless the land and waters;
give the world a plentiful harvest;
let your Spirit go forth
to renew the face of the earth.

As you show your love and kindness
in the bounty of the land and sea,
save us from selfish use of your gifts,
so that women and men everywhere
may give you thanks, for Jesus' sake. Amen.

—Holden Village, Chelan, Wash.

## 305  Fruits of the Earth

We pause to give you thanks, our Father,
>for the fruits of the earth
>given as a token of your love and care for us.

We pray you, grant that as we eat of this food,
>our bodies may be strengthened;

and that as we fellowship together,
>we might be mutually benefited
>and your name honored and glorified.

To this end, bless us and make us a blessing,
>for Jesus' sake, in whose name we pray. Amen.

—Cara Ulrich, in *Prayers for Everyday*, compiled by Elaine Sommers Rich (Newton, Kan.: Faith & Life Press, 1992), 34 (adapted)

# More Prayers

# Index for Worship Use

# Topical Index

# Scripture Index

# The Editor

Arlene M. Mark has been a writer from childhood and became a seminary student after her children were in school. Worship and liturgy became her focus when she was asked to serve on her congregation's worship commission and as a worship leader on Sunday mornings. That led to preparing worship materials for use in her congregation.

Mark challenged the editor of the Mennonite Publishing House bulletins to print worship resources on the bulletin backs that could be used in weekly worship services. The editor offered her a writing assignment. Over the years, there were many more. Eventually, a request came for her material and other selected pieces to be gathered into this volume, *Words for Worship*.

In 1982, Faith & Life Press and Mennonite Publishing House released *Worship Resources*, which Mark edited. In the Mennonite Church, she has led workshops on many facets of worship.

Arlene M. Mark lives in Elkhart, Indiana, with her physician husband, George. They are members of Prairie Street Mennonite Church, and she has served as its moderator. They have raised four children and cherish five grandchildren. She has taught school, serves on various boards both in the denomination and the community, and continues to write. Her hobbies include discovering and refinishing antiques, working crossword puzzles, and exploring new recipes.

# Notes